The Seen and
Teacher

David J Golden

Contents

Acknowledgments.. i

About the Author ii

Foreword x

Chapter 1: Have We All Got Psychic Powers?................... 1

Chapter 2: Psychic Powers.. 8

Chapter 3: Preparing a Meditation Room 13

Chapter 4: Meditation 18

Chapter 5: The Human Aura... 29

Chapter 6: How to Detect the Aura................................... 33

Chapter 7: Sexual Polarity and Mediumship 45

Chapter 8: Mediumship.. 52

Chapter 9: Preparing for a Demonstration of Mediumship
.... 71

Chapter 10: Mental Mediumship 77

Chapter 11: Public Speaking... 84

Chapter 12: Third Eye (Known as the Mind's Eye) 97

Chapter 13: Paranormal Activities Explained................. 103

Chapter 14: My Spiritual Diary 113

Chapter 15: God is Love (Creator of the Universe)........ 239

Chapter 16: Automatic Writing with Spirit Ron Baker .. 243

Acknowledgments

I would like to thank my beautiful partner Jacqueline Higgins for her encouragement to finish this book and for her support throughout this long journey. Her kindness shines like a beacon of light, helping a lost soul to find its way.

I wrote the book for those spiritual people who seek guidance and help with their spiritual journey. If one mortal soul can be encouraged to investigate their psychic energies, then it has been worth writing this small book.

I dedicate this book to Mr Ian Noble and Joyce Heppel, who became my spiritual inspiration. Two dedicated, loving, caring spiritual people who never had a bad comment about anyone. They both helped and advised me throughout our time together. In spirit, they still watch over me from their place of abode, making sure my spiritual knowledge increases every day. I can hear Joyce's voice now as I type, "Stop swinging your glasses by the arm, they will break." Yes, I still do.

About the Author

I was born on the 25th of December 1960 in Greater Manchester. Educated at a Roman Catholic School. Due to life circumstances at the time, I hardly attended school, which affected my education in all subjects. Over the years, I taught myself to read and write, which was quite difficult for me. Writing this book became a challenging task, but I knew I had to try, as I felt inspired by my spirit helpers. Let's begin!

I was extremely sensitive as a child and was subjected to all types of spirit phenomena. I believe we are all God's children, and he does not judge us. We all have free will and should be able to choose our own beliefs without being dictated to. During much religious instruction, I could not understand why `God` should make people suffer, and I questioned this! A few people were upset with me: for not mentioning any names. I took a complete break from Roman Catholicism to search for my own understanding: I always believed in God in what concept I did not know, but I knew deep down I was a nice person who liked everyone. When an unexplained occurrence happened, I buried my head and did not tell anyone of my experiences. But I never felt threatened or had any fear. I was more afraid of my own shadow than anything else.

After a long time of what I know now was my spirit family, looking after me and protecting me, even though I did not understand. In those days, it was a topic of taboo and deemed as evil, and I was not going to say it to anyone. Can you imagine what people would think of me? Anyway, I put it in the back of my mind and tried to get on with my life. Surviving was my first thought.

A spiritual inspiration came to my mind, and that was to visit Egypt over the period of Christmas 2009, travelling alone. I was booked in the Red Sea Resort Hotel, Hurghada, for two weeks. Each night I would meditate for one hour without fail. I had some wonderful spiritual experiences, and sometimes I thought it was my imagination.

On one occasion, after meditation, the thought of visiting the Great Pyramids, which I was told were 700 miles away from my location, and there were no trips scheduled to visit, with it being the Christmas period. I just knew I had to visit them, and not being perturbed early morning on New Year's Eve, I left the hotel with my rucksack and began to hitchhike across Egypt. I got into a small white van which was crowded with the locals. There was a language barrier, so most of the travel, I sat quietly. I had a feeling no harm would come to me throughout the journey, and I learned that the vehicle would be travelling back on the same day and that I could travel back with them. I had the sense these people were looking after me and making sure I was settled. They offered a bag full of nuts. I thought about how kind these strangers were to me, then I relaxed and enjoyed the journey. After a few hours on the road (dirt track), we stopped at a checkpoint. I noticed guys were carrying AK47 rifles, and they beckoned for us to get out of the van. Instantly the security knew I was not a local and searched my rucksack. They looked at me for a moment then pointed for me to get back into the van, which I did quickly.

Arriving in Giza, I had my first glimpse of the Great Pyramids, awesome sight. My body tingled from head to toe. The Great pyramid structure belonging to King Khafre, at the same time an electrical charge rushed through my body, and a thought entered my mind I needed to get inside the tomb.

I noticed an Egyptian guard standing at an entry point to the Great Pyramid. I gave him some money, and he let me go inside. I remember walking in a tunnel-like walkway that go steeper and smaller. There was a square entry point at the top. I climbed through into what appeared to be a chamber. My eyes adjusted slight, and I could make out where the base for the tomb was positioned. I scrambled across the dark ground and sat in the corner facing the tomb base. I closed my eyes and began to meditate. Seconds had passed, and I opened my eyes for a moment, and staring at me was a pair of eyes staring at me, hazel in colour they seemed. I quickly checked around the chamber to see if someone else was in the room, but no other physical person was in the chamber. I sat in amazement at what experience I had, and a thought entered my mind. I felt at peace and relaxed, and I felt this spirit entity was happy and at peace.

I made my way back to the entrance of the pyramid, letting my eyes adjust. I noticed the cloud looked as if they were pulling away from the pyramid. I experienced something quite special. I felt relaxed and happy and had an overwhelming sense of contentment. I located my transport the small white van, which the driver was waiting for me, and we all headed back to Hurghada, arriving ten minutes before midnight.

I spent several years demonstrating my spiritual gift at spiritual centres and churches throughout the Northwest of England. I found myself in spirit camps in America, providing private readings and as a public speaker.

There has been a time whereby I found myself in a deep trance state, which allowed the spirit communicator to come forward to provide a message to a recipient and to bring some spiritual knowledge by answering questions from the audience.

David knows it's an honour to represent the spiritual teachers, and he will continue to do so until spirit informs him it's time for another direction. On many occasions, David has helped the bereaved providing them with evidence to suggest eternal life, also those who seek spiritual knowledge.

I am today a practising spiritual medium, and I continue to read a spiritual book written in the early days, which I find spiritual culture to have been at its best. I would never force my belief on anyone. However, if they show an interest and ask, I am more than willing to help. I try to lead my life in the best possible way and have respect, and be honest.

However, like you, I am human and make mistakes, but I try to put these mistakes right. Some I can, some I cannot. It is never my intention to upset or harm anyone. If I did the opposite, then I am sure my spiritual life would not be as it is.

I have travelled extensively during my life, helping others who need help. I have done this from an early age, even though I did not realise it. You must have respect learn to know who you are and not what others want you to be. Being in touch with your inner self is the start of something wonderful.

I realised no matter where I was in the world, there was someone suffering, and they needed help. On many occasions, I have helped people of all cultures care for animals. To learn this is humanity as we are all connected, selfish people will never know their true value of life.

When you read my spiritual culture rules below, digest them, as simple as they are, but they are powerful words.

1. Be contented with the past and all it has brought you

2. Be thankful for the present and all you have

3. Be patient for the future and for all it promises to bring you

4. Love one another

5. Respect one another

6. Be kind to one another

7. Be at peace with all

8. Let the light within you shine bright

9. Self-analyse

10. Learn to forgive

11. Believe in yourself

12. Open your mind

I receive a spiritual quote during my deep meditation. I share this quote with everyone who I feel inspired to do so. I sense it is a message within itself for those who need that upliftment.

"Happiness is only a smile away."

I do not travel to conduct spiritual services because I have the sense of a slight change in my direction. The wonderful internet has brought the people of the world closer in the form of communication, where now you can see one another talk to one another, no matter where they are in the world.

Therefore, I enjoy writing spiritual/psychic emails and conduct one to one private live video readings. I read for people in different countries, and those people I believe are guided to me by their inner spirit. It shows that we are all children of the earth's core. Part of the universal law and the law of attraction.

Disclaimer

All the material contained in this book is provided for educational and informational purposes only. No responsibility can be taken for any results or outcomes resulting from the use of this material.

While every attempt has been made to provide information that is both accurate and effective, the author does not assume any responsibility for the accuracy or use/misuse of this information.

Foreword

Anyone can sit for development, providing they are of sound mind. The physical impediment is no barrier to development; however, common sense tells us that it can do no harm to be fit and healthy.

Looking at any development circle will tell you that those present are likely to be drawn from all walks of life within the circle; everyone is treated as equal. Anybody that wishes to develop must be prepared to put their own ego to one side, sit with humility and leave their personal problems at the door. There is no room for any form of prejudice whatsoever within any development class. If there is, then the development will break down.

This book is based on an ordinary man who leads his life in the best way he can. He learned how to control his psychic gift, and now he would like to share his experiences with you. You will find the book content easy to read and provide you with spiritual knowledge and answer some of those questions that you may have.

It's a book for those who are serious about becoming a spiritual medium or a psychic and about understanding all aspects of this amazing psychic gift. You will need a lot of patience during your development because there will be some highs and lows to the point you feel your unseen hosts are not teaching you anymore but be assured they will always work with you if you are willing.

I remember this happening to me. The reason why this happened is that it's part of their teachings, in other words letting you digest what you have been taught. It's like going back to school, but more in a relaxed state.

Chapter fourteen of the book is my spiritual diary showing the events of spiritual teachings. At the time, I had no idea this was going to be published. I followed their instruction and took notes without any questions. I am sure you will gain some spiritual knowledge and what to expect. You will understand how my spirit teachers taught me, how they prepared my mind, and how they cleared my mind of "Junk". My mind started to understand all life forms and what role they played on earth. We have one thing in common, "Energy". Before I could start to learn about spirit communication, I had to understand myself and learn about myself. They taught me how to accept my spirit, which is part of the physical body.

There are many subjects in this book to provide you with information regarding your spiritual journey or how to develop your psychic gift, which is also known as "Sixth Sense". The most important learning curve for any development is to have an open mind, and, in this book, you will find information that will point you in the direction to continue with your research.

You will also learn how to set up a meditation room. Basically, you are embarking on everything you need to know regarding working for the unseen hosts and how to identify spirit communication. Your mind will be prepared, and you will have some idea of what to expect as a working spirit medium. There are different types of spirit mediums that are explained. You will be able to identify which type of medium you will be.

I have covered in a chapter about "public speaking", which is an important part of spirit mediums working on stage. It explains how to build your confidence and what you are likely to expect when working in public. This is a very hard role to play, and some people find it difficult while others are natural at speaking in public. You must learn to relax your body and mind because it is the time when the spirit is able to draw close without any impediment.

There are other interesting subjects like "Sexual Polarity and Mediumship". This gives us some understanding when working with different energies, for example, male and female. Another interesting topic is "Paranormal Activity". As a psychic spirit medium, you will need to have some understanding of this subject. In this book, you will gain an insight into paranormal activity.

Have an open mind when reading this book, and you will find the information to be understandable and clear. Yes, by all means, question parts of the book you cannot understand or if it does not make sense to you. You can always send me a message regarding your concerns.

Working on behalf of spirit does not give you the right to use your sixth sense to manipulate others, and you should always respect other people's views. Learning to understand your sixth sense is a long process that cannot be rushed, in my opinion.

If you read this book at a steady learning pace and understand all the content, then you will be on your way to a new sense of feeling and a new life. You will find inner peace and learn how to control the stresses of the day. You will become in tune with your inner self, and above all, you will learn and understand the spirit within.

The book will teach you that ego plays no part when working for the spirit; however, you will find that you will become more sensitive and emotional. You will learn not to be judgemental towards others and have respect for all.

We are all moving, energy creating forces, and we must realise this energy is not only the unemotional abstract with which physicists are concerned. The energy of the divine outpouring is the energy of the divine desire, and we call it desire because we can only begin to understand the nature of the creative energy when we relate it to its nearest parallel in terms of human experience. For the sake of clarity, we discriminate between physical energy, emotion, thought and psychic energy, but we always need to bear in mind that all these are modes of the one creative outpouring. The psychic energies of our desires and emotions have an affinity with, belong to, and directly affect the subtle fields of desire. Everything we experience as feeling and desire, whether coarse or refined, corresponds to and is expressed as currents or disturbances within that watery realm. Our psychic integration is complexes of desired energy that we build around ourselves during our lives and that remain around us after physical death. Following the physical death, there is another `death`, for, after a variable period of etheric existence, the central core again withdraws, leaving the vortex empty. This empty vortex is now the 'astral shell' of spiritual and integration of the desired energies around an empty centre. Just as the physical body retains its form after death, so does the subtle vortex, and just as the one is subject to decay, so is the other; the former by those energy transformations known as bacteriological action, the latter by an action we can symbolise as a slowing down and gradual dissolution of the vortex, a dissolution into a magma of indiscrete tendencies.

There is a lot of spiritual knowledge in this book that will help you along your journey. Remember, it is for guidance only, and eventually, you will find the best way to utilise the spiritual information for your benefit.

The book will also provide valuable spiritual knowledge for those who want to broaden their spiritual experience and to give you an idea of the mechanics of developing a psychic sense. You may well find answers to some of your questions. Whatever your thoughts, I hope you enjoy what you read. "You can feel the wind, but you cannot see it."

Please understand this is a book for guidance only.

Chapter 1: Have We All Got Psychic Powers?

I believe everyone is psychic to some extent. It is just that some people are not open to their abilities like those people who are aware of their psychic gift. For a lot of people, this takes time to open to their own unique potential in becoming psychically aware. You need to truly recognise your potential in awareness, and most of all, you need to continuously practice at it and use these abilities as often as you can. Well, it is more common than we realise and that everyone is at least potentially psychic. Psychic is becoming more and more common these days because everyone is looking for that answer; 'what happens after death.' You don't need to look too far away, why, because you have the answer within you. In the whole psychic field, popular credence does not wait on facts but rather upon a supportive acceptance hypothesis as to the nature of man and matter. If all these hints, nudges and conclusions mediated by discarnate friends are in the right direction, then latently, everyone is psychic. The reach of the mind, which we all call paranormal or psychic, seems to me to have a good deal to do with life's dimension. We all can live constructed lives, or we can learn to see through and beyond appearances. This wider comprehension is thrust upon us after death, but it lies within our power now.

Does everyone have some psychic ability? I have thought about this fact. If psychic is so immensely useful, why is it not a common natural ability?

My conclusion is that it's more common than we realise that everyone at least has psychic potential. Let's look at this in more detail. People find themselves not believing anything they do not understand, and the psychic phenomenon is one of those subjects that a lot of people have no knowledge or limited information about. I have found that many sceptical people always come to their own conclusions and quickly disregard anything that seems to be out of their control. Society has informed us that we are not allowed to look and think for ourselves. Why? I don't know! Your guess is as good as mine, but for some reason, it seems to be that way. At one time in the earlier years, people did not believe that we could use technology to transmit and receive sound around the world. We were led to believe that the world was flat and, in fact, it is round. We would never have thought that one day we would be able to use the telephone to speak to someone on the other side of the world or watch a TV programme or listen to a radio being broadcast from another country. It is best to find information about something that we don't understand, and the psychic phenomenon is no exception.

Have you ever felt that someone is near or behind you; you look around to find nobody is there? Have you seen a small image at the corner of your eye, and when you turn towards the image, you cannot see it? No doubt there have been times when you have felt uncomfortable around strange people or in a strange room. You have that feeling that things are not right. Have you thought about someone that you have not spoken to for a while, next thing you hear from them? Have you thought about the telephone and a name of a person who you have not spoken to for a while? The telephone rings, and it's the person you have just thought about. It has been documented mothers know if there is something wrong with their children before anything is mentioned.

Have you had what is termed; 'da-jar-vu', been somewhere or seen someone, and you instantly say to yourself, I have been here before or seen them before? I would say that everyone at some stage in their life has had these thoughts, happenings they could not understand at the time. They could not find an explanation for these strange occurrences, and our senses could not relate to them. We tend to put these occurrences at the back of our minds and ignore them. Why have we had these experiences? I believe these are your psychic abilities, your sixth sense making you aware. And if developed, your sixth sense can produce wonderful experiences for you. It might even take away that fear of death or provide you with an understanding; after all, we all believe it is something. Understanding your psychic side will eliminate all your fears about the unexplained and of all the tabloids fictions stories of ghosts and zombies.

If we don't understand something, we automatically reject it instead of researching and finding your answers to those questions that keep on repeating themselves. Having a psychic gift can help you with your everyday life, making you more aware of things around you, and it will help you to avoid the difficult situations that you may come across. I believe our instincts are part of our psychic gift, and it plays a role in our life. You are like a receiver, and spirits are transmitters of information, and they send their thoughts in the form of telepathy. If you want to listen to a particular station on the radio, you use the tuning dial. Like a radio, you can finely tune yourself to the frequency of spirit communication, and with practice, you will find your link will become stronger. I believe meditation plays a vital role in this procedure, and it will help you to increase your vibration by relaxing the mind and body.

There are some excellent psychics who do not demonstrate their gift to the public, and they have a remarkable strong link with the spirit world. Having a psychic gift, a link to the unseen guest, can help and guide you along your pathway of life on the earth.

Today we need all the help we can get to be happy and stress-free, and if you listen to your psychic sense communicating with you, you will find that you don't make many mistakes. I am no exception to the rule! Many times, I have been aware that I should not have done something or be somewhere because my psychic sense has told me beforehand. Just like everybody else, I did not follow my first instinct and guess what? I made the wrong mistake or decision. Let me explain! Just before you shut the front door of your house, a thought enters your mind saying, "You have left your keys" you shut the door. You arrived back from the shops, walked to your front door, and remembered your keys were inside. Your psychic mind told you before you closed the front door, your keys were inside. The number of times I have found myself in similar situations, well, I have lost count. That thought is your initial instinct trying to warn you about your keys. You are being guided by your spirit mind. Another form of psychic powers is; when a family member or a friend, even a work colleague, asks you for advice regarding an important decision, and now you do not know the answer. You say to them, let me sleep on it, and I will tell you in the morning. How can you think about the decision when you are asleep? This used to confuse me until I learned and understood. Let me explain! We sleep to rest our physical body, and during our sleep state, our bodies repair and build up the energies ready for the next day. During our sleep time, we are not aware of what's happening in the physical world. In a sleep state, our spirit mind communicates with our spiritual family, and they help us with the decision. We usually wake up with a positive mind and an answer about the decision. The point I'm trying to put to you is to follow your first thought, and I can assure you you will find making decisions a lot easier.

Some people seem to think because they are blessed with psychic powers, they are special, and a little further up the ladder towards the realms of the Divine Source, this is far from the truth. People who are aware of their psychic abilities are no different from people who are not aware, and having psychic abilities does not make you a saint or have special powers. You still must abide by the laws of nature and help the progression of all life forms; we are all equal, nobody is better than anybody else. However, if you are aware of your psychic gift, then you are a privileged person. You may have experienced some sort of psychic phenomena but had no understanding.

Your psychic sense would have been stronger as an infant due to your innocents of life, and as we grow older, this sixth sense diminishes because we are introduced to new things in life, the material, stresses, and lifestyle. There are distractions, for example, televisions, computer games, alcohol, and many other distractions.

In the days of our elders, they entertained themselves by reading, singing, and dancing. They created a happy family atmosphere, which enabled the spirits to draw close and impress on the mind of family members. Physical Mediumship was at its highest because the conditions were a lot more favourable. In today's society, we are forever rushing around worrying about our life situations, which of course, is part of today's society. You have a sixth sense; maybe you cannot recognise it now. Think about it, have you at any time had something happen to you which does make sense. I am not saying you must be a psychic or a spirit medium to be a gifted person. We are all spirit, and our physical body is like an overcoat covering our spirit body. The physical body is a vehicle of expression whilst we are on the earth. This manual will provide you with some knowledge about your psychic side and help you to develop your inner senses.

Chapter 2: Psychic Powers

This hidden power is available to those who recognise and accept that there is a higher realm of knowing and communication beyond their own physical bodies. The universe is full of this unlimited energy that can be focused by anyone who will make an effort to focus and tune themselves to its subtle vibrations. These vibrations are not just for the 'spirit mediums or psychics' but for everyone who takes the time to learn. Most spirit mediums/psychics are that because they recognised the signs of this energy and focused their attention on its workings which is the very thing that is required to develop it. If they hadn't focused their attention on it, then they wouldn't be what they are. To begin tuning into this force, you need to learn about focusing on these vibrations. Focus on the slightest of psychic phenomena that happens to you or to people around you. Play the event around in your mind repeatedly to get familiar with the sense of the action and presence of the energies involved. This will provide you with a perception of how involved and integrated the underlying hidden power that caused the event to take place.

One of the most important things that you need to understand is that every living thing has consciousness and has a connection to everything else in the universe. People, animals, and plants are all connected to the hidden energy of universal consciousness (Law) that permeates the entire universe and places all of us together. When you understand and accept this concept as the most important requirement to develop one's own latent ability. The next important requirement is that you must have both a desire and willingness to develop and tune yourself so you can also connect with your spirit helpers. It becomes a matter of adopting a certain kind of mindset that is necessary to cultivate a power thinking process. Next, you will need to practice several exercise techniques diligently to get feedback while developing your abilities. Feedback helps you to learn and understand the signals and symbols that are received and experienced.

You will need to find a development circle or start a "circle" of your own. A circle means weekly meetings where like-minded people can practice in a positive environment. There you'll find tests and practices which will help you to begin developing your latent psychic abilities. They are not games but rather exercise for someone who is serious about psychic mind development.

Spiritual growth is the by-product of psychic development. As you expand your own awareness of the universe through the experiences you get from these practices, you will become more balanced and discerning. You will look at the world and people from a different perspective. You'll look at things rather than from their individual parts. You will have greater empathy because you'll understand what is happening around others, even if they don't see it themselves.

Each day of our lives, we experience some sort of paranormal practice, communicating with a higher realm of consciousness, and we are not even aware of it. I have listed experiences below that everyone has experienced at least once. Look them over and remember similar psychic events that happened to you. Once you have become aware of them, practice them, and more will occur. Through a higher awareness, you can make the paranormal become normal for you.

Pay attention to what is going on around you in everyday occurrences. When you experience one of the events listed below, write it in a book or a diary that you keep just for that purpose. Recording these events, no matter how trivial they may seem, will help you with your psychic development. Be sure to track your personal growth as well as psychic events.

Here are a few types of events.

1) Coincidences - Pay attention to coincidences that amaze you, including those that don't. All coincidences have a meaning; they may help you on your psychic or spiritual path. I suggest you record all of them.

2) Hunches - See what happens with your hunches. Take the effort to see if they play out as they came to you.

3) Urges - Follow up on urges. If you followed the urge, what happened?

4) The inner voice - Listen to it. Deep within, it gives you an awareness and knowledge about yourself or someone else. We don't always hear it because our conscious minds are preoccupied with ourselves. The subtlety of this voice sometimes makes us think that our mind is talking to itself. I suggest you record these occasions because this practice will help your ability to hear more of this voice.

5) Predictions- Have you spoken to someone on the telephone and tried to visualise what they look like or maybe going to meet someone for the first time and try to visualise them. Maybe you have visualised somewhere that you have never seen or been to, and your visions were accurate.

6) Senses - feelings that you are aware of when you enter a room full of people or meet someone for the first time. Knowing that thing is not right at the time of entering the room full of people or meeting that person, you become uncomfortable around them.

Simple as they seem, these points are the basics for developing your psychic gift. It will give you a tremendous amount of encouragement; in turn, your confidence will build up very fast. You will start to feel calmer and relaxed in your daily life and develop a keenness for more.

I say even at this very early stage, **DON'T RUSH!**

Chapter 3: Preparing a Meditation Room

Under certain known and reasonable conditions of temperature, light, etc., entities, existing in a sphere outside our own, have been demonstrated again and again to manifest themselves on earth in temporary bodies materialised from an, at present, undiscovered source, through the agency of certain persons of both sexes, termed sensitive and can be so demonstrated to any person who will provide the conditions proved to be necessary for such a demonstration.

As without conditions of some kind, no spiritual progress can be produced, any more than a scientific experiment, such as mixing various chemicals together to produce a certain result, cannot be carried out successfully without proper conditions being provided by the experimenter. What, then, do we mean by the word "conditions"?

Take a homely example. The baker mixes exactly the right quantities of flour, salt, and yeast with water and then places the "dough" which he has made in an oven heated to just the right temperature and produces a loaf of bread. Why? The conditions were good ones. Had he omitted the flour, the yeast, or the water, or had he used an oven over or under-heated, he could not have produced an edible loaf of bread because the conditions made it impossible. This is what is meant by the terms "Good conditions" "Breaking conditions." The conditions, then, under which I have been able to prove to many people that it is possible for quality spirit messages:

First: Light of suitable wavelength (suitable colour). A good light should be used during the whole time that the experiment lasts. I find that sunlight, electric light, gas, colza oil, and paraffin are all apt to check the production of the phenomena unless filtered through canary yellow, orange, or red linen or paper just as they are filtered for photographic purposes, owing to the violent action of the actinic (blue) rays which they contain (the rays from the violet end of the spectrum), which are said to work at about six hundred billion of vibrations per second. But if the light is filtered, in the way that I have described, the production of the phenomena will commence at once, the vibrations of the interfering rays being reduced; it is said, to about four hundred billion per second or less. Heat, electricity, and light, as Sir William Crookes tells us, are all closely related: we know the awful power of heat and electricity but are only too apt to forget, especially if it suits our purpose to do so. Light too has enormous dynamic potency; its vibrations being said to travel in space at the incredible speed of twelve million miles a minute; (186,900 miles a second, J. Wallace Stewart, B.S.C), and it is therefore only reasonable to assume that the power of these vibrations may be sufficient to interfere seriously with the more subtle forces, such as those which we are now investigating.

Secondly: We require suitable heat vibrations, and I find that those given off in a room either warmed or chilled to sixty-three degrees are the very best possible; anything either much above this or, more especially, much below this, tending to weaken the results and to check the phenomena.

Thirdly: we require suitable musical vibrations, and after carrying out a long series of experiments with musical instruments of all kinds; soothing music played on any disc player are most suitable, the peculiar quality of the vibrations given off by these instruments proving to be the most suitable ones for use during the production of the phenomena, although I have obtained good results without musical vibrations of any kind.

Fourthly: The room needs to be well ventilated with a steady flow of fresh air, and the furniture needs to be all wooden, dark wood if possible. A suitable table made of light-dark wood should be placed in the centre of the room. For flooring, I suggest a laminate floor that would not absorb the energy and the walls decorated with white wallpaper to reduce any false impressions.

I use my outside building (brick built shed), which is ideal for my meditation room. I am the only person with a key. There is plenty of fresh air that enters the room and, in the darkness, there is no natural light entering the room whatsoever. You could build a wooden shed if you have the room in your garden, again this will be ideal. Some people use their spare room in their homes for meditation.

I always state it's wise to make sure the door is locked to stop someone from entering the room whilst the meditation is in progress. A suitable timing device that will make sure you do not meditate for long periods. After a while, you will automatically come back to consciousness by your body's timing senses.

You should always start your meditation on the same day and at the same time; to allow the energy in the room to create and, if possible, keep this room always locked to stop other people from entering. This room should be for meditation purposes only. I understand that not all students will have a spare room in their home to use for meditation only. However, you can make the most of a room, let's say the bedroom, for temporary purposes.

Your meditation room, after some time, will become your sanctuary where you will find peace and calm. All the day's stresses will be left at the door. I often find myself sitting in my meditation room reading one of my spiritual books whilst listening to music. Not any music, but the music I like. Often than not, I slowly drift off, knowing the spirits are with me, touching my face and sensing their presence.

Chapter 4: Meditation

Meditation is the handmaiden of prayer, and the two are so subtly connected and interrelated that it is difficult to separate them. We are mainly concerned with a form of meditation directed towards producing a state of mind conducive to all spiritual and mediumistic activity rather than those forms which tend towards the development of the self to rise above worldly conditions. I have always felt that the true aspirant serves no purpose in sitting upon the mountain of self-illumination completely out of touch with those passing through the valley that needs help.

All religions have produced their mystics who seemingly transcend the mundane religious concepts and emerge upon a level of consciousness, linking them automatically to all others who have achieved a similar position regardless of the different religious paths traversed. It is perhaps ironic that these mystics are mostly ostracised by the religion which they love. We must realise that all religions lying side by side are the twin pathways of theology and mysticism. It is interesting to observe in the Aquarian Age that the pathway of theology is less crowded, and more and more people are turning towards mysticism.

In meditation, we endeavour to turn our thoughts and energy inward upon ourselves in an attempt to illuminate the state of consciousness by the power of spiritual vision, which must not be confused with clairvoyance. It has often been said that the spirit teacher appears, but ultimately, we shall find that, as the indwelling spirit floods the personality with divine love and light, bringing into subjection the negative elements, the teacher referred to is not just another individual but the indwelling spirit whose luminosity has started to energise the spiritual potential. It has been more adequately expressed in terms of `YOGA`, as the awaking of the `Kundalini` or serpent power.

In my experience, many students of meditation are misled by concepts of peace and tranquillity in connection with meditation, whereas in early attempts, the mind is almost invariably in a state of turmoil and conflict. The practise of meditation is not achieved by a blank and empty mind, which in any case is quite an impossible feat, but rather it is aimed towards an examination of those fleeting images which together constitute the person. We must be prepared, therefore, in the early stages, to see many things which are offensive and hurtful to our personal dignity, but we must always remember that these images of conflict represent our true state of being.

The first rule to remember is that a great deal of time will be spent in carefully examining and analysing all the rubbish which has been stored in mind without any conscious effort and to which perhaps we would rather turn a blind eye. It is imperative, therefore, that the student accepts the fact that, before meditation can bring its own special illumination, the rough and dirty work of cleaning the house must first be conducted in a cheerful and energetic manner, in readiness for the anticipated spiritual changes to take place. Any attempt to dismiss unwanted thoughts from you will simply have the effect of making them more potent. It is vital that all thoughts should be carefully examined and analysed before being relegated to their respective departments in the memory. Eventually, through this discipline, proper control over the memory and imagination will be achieved, and during meditation, unwanted thought images will no longer appear beckoned upon the screen of the mind. This is the first step towards mastery over the mind, which, in its untrained state, evokes the analogy of a seething atomic reactor and meditation on how it is controlled and its energy directed in a purposeful manner.

My earliest attempts at meditation as an aspirant spirit medium were most successful only when the mind was occupied with an external image. I would go out into the countryside and walk along a pathway over the hills taking in every detail of nature. I would stop at a particular tree and embrace it with both arms. The energy and strength and the warmth from the tree wrapped around me like a blanket of protection, providing me with contentment and strength.

I would say a semi-hypnotic state was probably achieved, which permitted spiritual inspiration to take place. In the creation myth of Brahma, who stood on a thousand-petalled lotus and cast his eyes to the four points of the compass, symbolising the need for spiritual orientation, the fundamental basis of meditation can be understood. Man is a four-legged being, possessing physical, mental, emotional, and spiritual propensities, and in the act of meditation, orientation towards his spiritual aspect is absolutely necessary. Awareness of spiritual orientation is achieved through service to others and our efforts to forward the Divine Purpose. Without this conscious effort on our part, spiritual orientation cannot be achieved, and therefore meditation would serve no purpose. In our everyday life, there must be a constant striving towards attunement with God which must bring about the desire's orientation. This cannot be achieved by meditation but truly depends entirely upon the way in which we live our lives. It must always be remembered that life is the result of inner energy manifesting outward and that the outward life is only a pale reflection of eternal life.

I tried numerous techniques of meditation with varying degrees of success. I now present the technique which I have adopted and which, although very simple, has proven to be very effective.

Before even attempting meditation, have several sessions simply learning how to sit still, the object being to move away from a conscious awareness of the physical body which must be in a placid and not active condition. The position of the body during meditation must be determined by the position in which it is most placid, regardless of what this is. Breathing is a very important part of meditation. Sit in an erect posture, keeping the spinal column straight and the eyes well to the front, letting the hands rest on the upper part of the legs.

Breathe rhythmically, but instead of breathing through both nostrils, press the left nostril close with the thumb, and inhale through the right nostril. Then remove the thumb and close the right nostril with the finger and then exhale through the left nostril. Then, without changing the fingers, inhale through the left nostril and change fingers, exhale through the right. Then inhale through right and exhale through left and so on, alternating nostrils as mentioned. This is one of the oldest forms of Yogi breathing and is quite important and valuable.

Direct the mind towards your particular concept of God and take a few deep, though not excessively deep, breaths, which will have the effect of informing the body and mind of what is about to take place. During meditation, the breathing invariably changes as it does in sleep, and this will happen quite automatically without any conscious effort being required. The first two points should occupy no more than approximately sixty seconds. The whole objective is that the meditation is under your control.

Meditation should always commence and end at the same point if only for the purpose of strengthening the visual images involved, consequently leaving more time available for actual meditation. Personally, I have created a mental reproduction of my walk in the countryside, which I can visualise at a moment's notice. I will examine any particular thought for which the meditation is being made and have found that this works equally well for absent healing, prayer, spiritual contemplation and even communication with loved ones from the spirit world. At the close of my meditation, I visualise that I am at the base of the tree.

I always open my meditation with a prayer. It does not have to be the Lord's Prayer. I have a conversation with the Divine Spirit, and to me, that's my prayer. You must always close with a prayer, meaning, at the end of your meditation, say a prayer. You are closing the door between the two worlds.

This technique is strengthened with each successive meditation and permits the separation of mind from the physical body in the act of going forward beyond the symbolic barrier of the wall. The student should aim at creating a visual picture to which they are able to respond in a joyful way and which they will always be eager to visualise. Obviously, a person who has a fear of water should never attempt in their visualisation to create a swift-running river but should choose surroundings in which they are completely relaxed and at peace with the world.

In presenting these thoughts upon mediation and prayer, I have tried to remove some of the mystery surrounding these subjects. I always feel that simple directions are often the most difficult to grasp. I highly recommend Yogi Breathing techniques, and the breathing technique I have mentioned, without doubt, has played a major part in my mediation. Life is dependent on breathing. "Breathing is life". To breathe is to live, and without breath, there is no life. All creatures are dependent on breath and health. Breathing may be considered the most important of all the functions of the body, for indeed, all the other functions depend upon it. A man may exist some time without eating, a shorter time without drinking, but without breathing, his existence may be measured by a few minutes. Correct breathing habits continued vitality and freedom from diseases. Intelligent control of our breathing power will lengthen our days upon the earth by giving us increased vitality and power of resistance, and on the other hand, unintelligent and careless breathing will tend to shorten our days by decreasing our vitality and laying us open to diseases.

I am sure the student will be able to research this method of breathing in more detail and find which is the best method of breathing that will be suited for you. This will take time to be patient. It is vital you select the best method of breathing. I am aware that we all have busy schedules, and we don't find the time to meditate. May I suggest that you find somewhere where you can relax and sit quietly for a few minutes, this could be at a coffee break, ironing, cleaning, before you read the newspaper or watch that favourite T.V programme. We all could make time for ourselves if we wanted to. If you are considering working for the spirit world, then you will have to take the time for meditation which helps your psychic powers.

Meditation is a purposely induced state where the physical body and conscious mind are bypassed temporarily, so the inner self comes into focus. Through a series of mental exercises, the body is placed at rest, and simultaneously, the mind is emptied of all thoughts enabling the person to create a sort of suspended animation. It is at this point that a state of pure heightened awareness without thought is attained.

Mystics of all religions have claimed that once this state is achieved, one can listen for God or all that is, to speak. The depth from which the psychic reader gets information is not quite as deep as this state, but practice makes it easier for the psychic to 'drop' into the level where all the psychic activity takes place. A big bonus for people who meditate is the enhanced health benefits they receive as a by-product.

When – I find starting meditation can be when you have free time during the day; for me, this is in the afternoon. It is a good idea to have an alarm to make you aware of when to stop mediating. Use this method until your psychological clock starts to let you know when it is the end of the meditation. You do not need to meditate every day, but one or two times per week is fine. You will find your own method of relaxing and meditation, so do not overthink about it.

Where - Find a place where you won't be disturbed by noises, telephones, or other people barging in on you. Sit upright either on the floor or in a straight-back chair with a cushion, so you are comfortable. Don't lie down on the bed; you may fall asleep. Unless you really find this position suitable for you. You will find, at first, it is hard not to fall asleep; most people fall asleep. In time you will learn to relax the mind and body without falling asleep.

The object of the process is twofold; to relax the body and to subdue the thoughts that continuously traverse our mind. You do this by occupying the mind with the process of relaxing the body. As the body relaxes, so does the mind. One never stops the mind completely, but one can achieve states of relatively long periods where the mind is silent. It is during these moments, no matter how brief they are, that we enter a state of the void, the null or nothingness. This is the state of being that the mystics refer to as listening to God.

The process is to sit in your selected place and relax. Take a few deep breathes, paying deliberate attention to the sound of the air as it enters and exits. Focus your mind on your body and begin instructing it to relax. Beginning at the top of your head, instruct the muscles to relax, and then actually feel these muscles relax. Move on to the face and neck muscles, focusing your mind on instructing your body to relax these muscles and then actually feeling the muscles relax before you go on. Continue doing this until you have reached your toes. Then you will be aware of the relaxed state your body is in.

If at any time your mind drifts onto something else, just return it back to the task of relaxing your body parts.

Don't fight or struggle against these thought intrusions. Just let them go peaceably away, and continue the process.

Once you have completed the body part, relaxation, and then begin to relax the mind. You do this by beginning to count backwards and paying attention to the actual numbers. This way, you occupy your mind with the process of meditation, leaving no room for extraneous thoughts to enter. This helps to train your mind to focus. Start the counting from around twenty, and imagine seeing the shape of each number as you count down. When you reach the bottom, start the count over again and when you reach the bottom again, repeat the process again. At one point, you may disappear from the counting process and not be aware that you've done so. It's OK, don't be concerned; it's part of meditation.

As you practice this process, you'll find that it gets easier to avoid the thoughts that are in your mind. Focus decreases the impact of random thoughts and allows you to drift into a state of nothingness. No matter how long you meditate, you will always have days when it seemed perfect and flawless, and then you will have those days that seem like bummers. It's also OK because what counts is the overall effect. After you have practised for a while, you will notice the difference in your life, and you'll wonder why you didn't start sooner. Remember to tell yourself, prior to starting each time, how much time you want to spend. Your inner clock will let you know when the time is up.

Chapter 5: The Human Aura

In Christian Art, important figures are depicted with luminosity surrounding the head and shoulders and other times encompassing the whole body, respectively known as nimbus and oral. Without a doubt, it was a representation of spiritual power. The colour classification would incorporate the Godhead, and Saints were generally Gold. The patriots Silver, whilst ordinary people were given halos of Red, Blue, Green and Violet. Evil beings were represented by black. The Gods of the Hindus and the founders of the Sikh religion were shown with the Halo whilst the profit of Islam is depicted holy as a flame, and Muslim Rulers were often shown with a flame around the head. Further examples may be found in the Egyptian, Roman, Greek, and Chinese together with numerous more obscure cultures.

Clairvoyance over the centuries have described subtle colour radiations seen emanating from the human body, but it is only recently that the subject has attained scientific status due to modern systematic methods of research and instrumentation. Mr Anton Mesmer, in the 1700s, announced his discovery of the animal magnetic fluid and all though his work fell into disrepute due to highly dramatic magnetic methods of treatment, he remains the pioneer in the modern world of this ancient subject. In 1845 Mr Baron Vonrightonback, a German Physicist, announced his discovery of radiation around the human body and coined the term odic force to describe the phenomena. He utilised the service of trained sensitive or mediums in his investigation and reported the auric radiations emanating from the poles of magnets. In 1920, Dr Kilner published his book, the human atmosphere giving details of his observations and research methods. However, the most dramatic discovery in recent years which employs high-frequency electrical currents was made in Russia. A Russian electrician notices that if his fingers were in a field of high frequencies currants and he touched a sheet of photographic paper, the impression of spots, lines and zigzags would appear on it. Later a microscope was incorporated, and in the high frequencies field, various colour lights shone against a dark background. Perhaps further discoveries will be made, entailing more advanced instrumentation in the future. Until then, however, the testimony of clairvoyance will provide the material for further investigation.

The aura appears to be electro-magnetic in nature and is affected by health or illness, emotions, thought, mentality, and spiritual evolution of the individual. Different researchers have described the auric fields, and as in all fields of human investigation, differences of opinion arise. The human aura is the energy field that surrounds the human body in all directions, and it is three dimensional. In healthy people, it makes an elliptical or egg shape around the body.

Everyone has an aura and has seen or experienced the auric field of others. People ignore the experience or chalk it up to something that it is not. Children are very good at seeing the aura, and at some time, they have experienced the aura. Those experiences are often translated into their drawings around figures; they will usually use the same colour that they have experienced. These colours often reflect the energies they have observed around the figure or of what they are drawing.

It is important that we maintain a balanced diet and try to avoid alcohol, drugs, tiredness, stress, and smoking. I believe our aura shows signs of illness or diseases before it enters our physical body, and one day our medical researchers will be able to detect these signs and be able to provide treatment before it enters the physical body. I have often seen within the aura, looks to be soft star lights. They are usually very sparkly and silver in colour. I have found that they indicate one of several things. "Stars," as I call them, are almost always a sign of great creativity and fertility. When they appear within the auric field of a person, it indicates greater is being activated within the person's life.

I can only report the conclusion of my own research and refer the student to the work from other authors upon the subject. I detect four auric fields, and they are as follows:

The Physical Aura – Extends approximately one inch in all directions around the physical body.

The Mental Aura – Encompasses the head.

The Etheric Aura – Extends approximately two feet at the centre.

The Spiritual Aura – Extends all around the individual.

Note: A portion of the aura that is seen by the average person is the physical aura because it is close to the normal spectrum.

Chapter 6: How to Detect the Aura

There are many methods of detecting the aura; Clairvoyant observation, it must be remembered that the aura is seen with the eyes of the etheric body and not with the physical eyesight, except in the case of the physical aura, which is close to the normal spectrum. The physical aura may be seen by placing the hands close together with fingers just touching against a black or dark background. Just gazes at the fingers without too much concentration, then slowly draw the fingers apart when the energy radiation may be seen, bridging the gap between the fingers. If you fail at two or three attempts, try the next day again. The ability to see in this way ebbs and flows and cannot be forced. It is far better to have fifty attempts on different days than to try hour after hour in vain. When the auric field has been recognised between the fingers, experiment next with the head. When listening to someone speaking, try to observe the auric radiation around the head and shoulders.

In order to see the complete aura with clairvoyance, it is best to sit opposite the subject of two to three feet, eyes closed with hands resting on the knees. Concentrate on the idea of the aura in mind and wait for the clairvoyant image to arrive. In practice, sometimes one of the four auric levels will appear, in which case simply ask mentally for the other levels, which will then often appear on the partially formed image. If the attempt is negative, try again later; never try to force clairvoyance which can only result in highly imaginative material, which is of no value and is often result in spoiling psychic ability. Individuals who can use a pendulum for dowsing work can often extend the faculty to order analysis, the subject is placed with the head to the magnetic north, and the pendulum is then used in the normal manner. It must be borne in mind; however, the positive and negative pull phenomena will be present. For example, at the top and base of the spine, the left and right lobes of the brain. The best method is probably that of mental orientation with the pendulum to plot the aura and establish the colour frequency present. Many individuals can sense the aura by using their own hands in much the same way has the pendulum is used. The operator simply adopts a passive mental state and passes the hand through the aura to register the radiation.

Those who can exercise the talent of psychometry may, with practice, be able to extend the faculty to auric analysis. In this case, it is essential to have a good sample, for example, a much-worn item that only belongs to the subject. Following your normal procedure, direct the mind to tune with the subject. This method is extremely useful but requires careful and disciplined development. I have also found that if you look through a flame (not staring at the flame), you will see the energy around the flame, and the flame will appear to lengthen. I would gaze at different animals, and eventually, their physical aura appeared. If you look along a country lane on a hot summer day, you can see the heat rising from the road; this is energy that the sun has created. Now, this same haze you see is like the aura sighting, but in colour.

Feeling the Aura and Energy

Learning to feel auras and energy fields with your hands is one of the most fundamental skills to acquire when learning to do any work with energy. Before you attempt to feel the aura, you must be relaxed and mentally visualise the aura. You will need to pay attention to the subtle changes you feel in your hands as you pass them several inches over a person. Some people feel in different ways; they feel the energy thermally, as changes in temperature. For these people, different areas of the aura will feel warmer or cooler, depending on what they are detecting.

I know one person who feels the heat as his hands pass over an injury or sickness in part of the body, while another friend feels cold when passing over the same location. They are detecting the same energy imbalance but perceiving it in different ways. How the energy is perceived is individual, but the energy that is being felt is real, tangible, and

35

verifiable. The best way to improve your skills is to work with a partner. What you and your partner should do is practice feeling each other's aura and reporting the sensations as you pass your hands a few inches around your partner. You should eventually be able to "work out" your partner's aura. The aura changes shape every day due to your emotions. As you practice, you will be picking up energy from each other because you are both practising being deliberately receptive. This is a great time to get in the habit of good spiritual hygiene. Always ground and cleanse yourself after working on one another and when healing other people. You need to remove all the negative energies from your aura after you have worked on each person. The aura is the field of energy that radiates from all matter. Living things produce more amounts of this radiant energy, so their auras are brighter and easier to see. The aura is most often "seen" with the "third eye" or the "inner eye". Some people seem to have the ability for seeing auras, other people find it hard, and they must work at developing this sight.

Auras display the colours of the rainbow and respond to the emotional and physical status of the body. There are many people who interpret the colours they see for a variety of purposes. The colours might detect an illness or reveal an emotional issue. However, different traditions disagree about the meanings of different colours seen. Therefore, the colours should be interpreted by the person who sees them.

Hold your hands out about two feet apart, palms facing each other. Slowly bring your hands together until they are about eight inches apart. Can you feel any changes? Slowly bring your hands closer until they are about two-three inches apart. At this point, you should feel like two magnets are trying to slightly repel each other. (Have you ever played with magnets and tried to get the wrong ends to match up? It's that sensation.) Bounce your hands together and along this "magnetic" zone, and you can really feel the auras bouncing off each other. Learning about the aura and being able to detect the aura will enhance your psychic skills and will, increase your knowledge and enable you to create a stronger link with spirits.

The Colour Rays

The solar spectrum or rainbow is obtained by the refraction of light through a prism. Each colour radiation has a spiritual meaning, and this is in turn modified by the degree of brightness and the level of manifestation within the aura. The story of Snow White and the Seven Dwarfs illustrates the different personality types according to colour classification (folklore of colour). Light has always been associated with goodness and darkness with evil or ignorance. The biblical command, 'Let your light shine before men, is really a directive to cultivate a spiritual approach to life which produces in the auric field the beautiful rainbow colours of the spiritually evolved. Every individual has this auric `robe of many colours', which tells the story of each life without error or mistake. It reveals what we really are and not what we think we are.

Your mood, what you're doing and what you're experiencing in life all determine the colours of your aura at any given time. The colours of your aura are, can be affected by the energies of other people. It is common to have other people's colours in your aura or their energies left in a building. There are many colour variations in the universe. So, it is a mistake to squeeze aura colours meaning down into a 'cut and dried' colour code. There are, however, some general themes that can help guide the interpretation process. Keep in mind aura colours' meaning depends on the shades and who the energy comes from. All aura colours have a different meaning at the time of reading, depending on the emotions of the recipient.

These are some rough guidelines for interpreting aura colours.

RED: A physical ray representing strength and vitality. Courage and leadership are also indicated when the ray is bright. If strong and of a darker tone, it reveals the materialistic personality given to fits of temper and suggests, ruled by the animal instincts and appetite. This ray is associated with the reproduction glands. Lifeforce, survival, raw passion, anger, frustration, determination, sense of importance, feeling overwhelmed by change.

ORANGE: This indicates a warm personality with an optimistic approach to life. The mind is alert and energetic. The ray tends to energise the other virtues in the aura and, when strong in the aura, often indicates sensitivity and sympathy towards others. It is easily transmitted in the form of energy, and people under the orange influence need to learn how to conserve energy. When the ray is of a darker tone, beware of pride and ruthless ambition.

It is associated with the adrenals and has been described in the past as the ray of vitality. Sensuality, physical pleasure, emotional, self-expression, creativity, lacking reason, health, and vitality are all related to it.

YELLOW: This ray gives a love of truth and the desire to learn. When strong, it indicates spiritual enfoldment as represented in art as the golden halo. There is a craving for spiritual food, and this colour is always found in spiritual teachers. Clairvoyants see this colour in the mental aura of inspirational speakers. All matters concerned with the communication of learning are represented in this ray. It is associated with the pancreas. The urge to learn and make progress often requires the virtue of patience. Mental alertness, analytical thought, happiness, optimism, childlike, ego-driven and thinking at the expense of feeling are all related to it.

GREEN: Versatility and creativity are revealed by this colour. It has excellent balancing properties and those under this influence grasp the situation quickly. As the middle ray of the spectrum, it is not surprising that the ability to `weight things up` is indicated, together with an analytical mind. You cannot rush anyone who has this ray strongly established due to the need for attention to detail. In the negative registration, envy and jealousy are indicated. It is associated with the thymus.

Healing, peace, nurturing, new growth, fear, need for security, jealousy and envy, and balance.

BLUE: The ray of inspiration has always been associated with the feminine qualities of love, peace, harmony, and protectiveness. Usually, it is well established in the aura of spiritual healers and all engaged in social work. There is a strong desire to help others, and high ideals are practised. When powerful in the aura, guard against the tendency to worry. It is associated with the thyroid. Verbal communication, free-thinking, relating to structure and organisation, possibilities, and spiritual intelligence are all related to it.

INDIGO: This indicates a loyal and sincere personality that is highly intuitive. It is the colour of deep spiritual conviction and has been much used in places of religious worship. Music lovers and those who appreciate solitude often develop this ray. It is also a good colour for meditation and prayer. In the negative registration, avoid introversion and the tendency to live in a dream world. It is associated with the pituitary. Wisdom, authoritative, female energies, matriarchal, sense of superiority, controlling, imagination, intuition

VIOLET: The highest ray in the spectrum. It indicates spiritual rebirth in the highest sense. I have never found this ray where ego rules the personality. It is to be found in the auras of mystics, seers, poets, and all engaged in the higher powers of the mind and in spiritual mediumship, where the psychic and mediumistic talent has been unfolded and moulded upon spiritual objective. A sense of loneliness is often experienced by the violet subject due to a lack of understanding of where the mediumistic temperament is concerned. It is associated with the pineal. These are just some of the colours that I have observed during my clairvoyance. Variations in colour meaning will arise from

41

person to person, and the descriptions given are by no means complete. They should be used as a guide only, and the serious student will soon be able to enlarge upon them.

Folklore and Colour

Purple with Passion: Describes the ultra-intensification of the physical aura in moments of acute emotional involvement.

A Touch of the Blues: When this colour is powerful in the aura, the subject is well-advised to avoid states of anxiety associated with concern for others.

This feminine attribute has been in the past with the material image.

Green with envy: Describes the negative aspect of this ray, and if established in the aura, remedial action is indicated.

A Yellow Streak: Describes the condition of cowardice. However, remembering the old saying `fools rush in where angels fear to tread, the true meaning is found. The wisdom aspect of the yellow-ray permits the recognition of danger which is often ignored by the foolish.

I saw Red: Describes the red tone of the aura in moments of anger.

In the Pink: Describes the light pink radiation of the physical aura in those blessed with good health and vitality.

Black follows Green: Describes the negation of colour in the aura, which is radiating the green tone of sickness, which could lead to physical death: hence the superstition of not hanging green curtains.

Many other examples will be found in local sayings, where the original auric interpretation has been obscured. The properties of the colour rays have been employed in `chromatic healing` or healing by colour. It is well known that some colours have a stimulating effect, and others may be soothing. The student who is interested in this aspect will find a rich field for research.

Because of a clairvoyant experience, I believe that a self-healing phenomenon takes place within the auric field where the disease is concerned and which involves polarisation of certain auric rays from the diseased part. Some years ago, engaged in spiritual teachings, I observed different shapes moving around the walls, floor of the room and around people with whom I was in contact.

These colourful shapes seem to be attracted to people and the outdoors. They would be visible to me, near trees flowers. Remember, all life form has an electromagnetic field in the form of the aura around them. Sometimes the

43

colourful shapes would be stationary, or they would move slowly, directly in front of me.

Chapter 7: Sexual Polarity and Mediumship

The law of duality is fundamental within the context of the known universe, and progress apparently depends upon a harmonious interchange between the various polarities. i.e., male/female, positive/negative, a principle which was recorded of old by the entry of the animals into the ark two by two and in science by our understanding of electrical and magnetic phenomena. The basic building blocks of matter. For example, the atom, with its positive and negative electrical charge, reveals this fundamental law which operates in the physical, mental and spiritual dimensions.

When the balance of harmonious interchange is disturbed, the effect is recognisable as in the human male/female polarity. Male-dominated society has resulted in aggression and war, a situation which can only be rectified by the feminine polarity of love. I believe that the human spirit is sexless but is sexually polarised by its vehicle of expression for a short part of the eternal journey. Hermaphrodites, in which the characteristics of both sexes are evident, could be the early sign of an evolutionary mutant, rather than a genetic 'throwback', a possibility which would require a complete restructuring of present concepts in relation to 'wholeness'. The sexual polarity functions beyond the physical dimension, and our illustrious seer A.J. Davis has attributed wisdom and love respectively to the male/female polarities. Although this may be oversimplified for present-day standards, it nevertheless draws to the law of duality and its harmonious interrelationship.

More profoundly, he states that God is the greatest fact in the universe, he is the greatest principle, and he is the greatest reality, the active or moving principle. God is active and moving. Nature is passive and moved. God is our father; nature is our mother, and we are their children. God is the great central source of all life and love, all order and form, the sustainers and enfolder of all things, the magnificent universe. God is the infinite cause; nature is the infinite effect.

The male personality has a subjective female polarity, as the female possesses a subjective male polarity. The balance of this androgynous `see-saw` is vital to physical, mental and spiritual equilibrium. Apparently, it is also directly involved in and affected by psychic and mediumistic activity or equally may provide how the phenomena are registered. `Poltergeist` activity is the exteriorisation of psychic energy from young adolescents, whose awakening sexuality forms the energy supply.

Historically, the many sexual taboos, including transvestite, seers, priests, etc., indicate the connections between mediumship and human polarity.

Scientifically, the mind is a mystery, and its function of consciousness is a void on the map of understanding. Spirit teachings, however, have provided a glimpse across the frontiers of knowledge and established guidelines for our benefit. The mind is the communicative part of the spirit, invisible except for its luminosity, which has been observed by clairvoyants for thousands of years and which is now the subject of scientific investigation. During the earth period of life, only a small part of the total mental potential can be utilised due to the limitations imposed by the physical brain and human sexual polarity. The subconscious levels may be understood as another aspect of the polarity phenomena, especially when we understand that mediumship utilises the unconscious or subjective mind, a fact which is true also in relation to dreams, where the subconscious impulses are registered at a conscious level, a state which is parallel to normal subjective mediumship. It follows, therefore, that the subconscious mind together with the subjective polarity is the source of mediumistic potential, also that the polarity is capable of tremendous change at physical death, leading eventually to the complete extinction of the subconscious barrier and to the state of `supernormal consciousness', when the full mental potential may be realised. I would theorise that only in this advanced state shall we be able to comprehend what the meaning of spiritual `wholeness` really is.

Spirit mentors have advised that in the spirit world, the mind is able to act directly upon its surroundings without the necessity of personal intervention by way of tools. An exercise that is constantly performed in dreams, where the dreamer can create and dissolve at will, in accordance with his/her thoughts patterns. Is the dreamer simply practising the use of full mind potential in preparation for the journey ahead? When viewed in this light, sexual polarity should, in my opinion, be the subject of vigorous investigation and research. A study of mediums will often reveal a strongly developed subjective nature, which may show as sensitivity and gentleness in males and masculine characteristics in females. A study of mediums will often reveal a strongly developed subjective nature, which may show as sensitivity and gentleness in males and masculine characteristics in females.

Some males wear earrings, hug each other tenderly and express a loving relationship. Some males take care of their children whilst their partner is at work. Some males show their emotional side when watching a sad movie.

Females have been involved in aggressive sports, change the oil in the car, and many females are good at do-it-yourself jobs. Just about anyone can animate either masculine or feminine energy at any moment.

I believe every spirit medium or psychic needs to be in touch with their subjective mind in order to sense or feel the communicating spirit of the opposite sex. If mediums are not conscious of their subjective minds, this will make it difficult for the spirit medium to say what type of sex the spirit communicator when they were in the physical body. For sexual polarity, you need an energetic polarity, an attractive difference between masculine and feminine. The male takes the feminine role sometimes, and the female takes the masculine role. I believe that we need to have access to both our essentials to be balanced and whole. You will find we do this without realising we do share these roles.

All-natural forces flow between two poles. The north and south poles of the earth create a force of magnetism. The positive and negative poles of a battery create an electrical flow. The masculine and feminine poles between people create a flow of sexual energy in motion. For the real passion for occurring, there needs to be a ravisher and a ravishee. Sexual polarity is not required for love, but it is necessary for sexual attraction in a relationship. A man may have a feminine core, and a female may have a masculine core, or

49

they could both be more balanced in their masculine and feminine aspects, but if one partner is willing to play the masculine polarity while the other plays the feminine polarity, they can enjoy sexual interaction with each other in a satisfying manner. The feminine is pure, boundless, and infinite energy moving freely without any particular direction. It is directionless but immense, ever-changing, beautiful and destructive. The feminine is the force of life and source of inspiration. The feminine moves in all directions, the masculine moves in one direction. The feminine needs the masculine to give it direction, focus and purpose. The masculine needs the energy of the feminine to give it drive and passion. The masculine and the feminine need each other. The masculine directs while the feminine projects. This is the relationship of yin and yang. The feminine looks to the masculine for direction. A woman does not want a man to look to her for direction but would rather he follow his own direction. It is better for a man to act when he wants to and not need a woman to give him permission to do as he pleases. A woman would rather a man acts when he feels like it instead of when she feels like it, and for him to be able to change her feelings at will. That is why a woman prefers a man to take the initiative in most things. She wants him to keep leading and advancing every step of the way instead of waiting without knowing what to do next.

You must animate the masculine and feminine differences if you want to understand the different types of spirit communicators.

I can understand that some people feel trapped in the wrong body; for example, a female trapped in her physical body when her mind suggest she should be a male and a male trapped in his masculine physical body when his mind suggests he should be a female. We should not criticise them but try to understand these people, and I am sure we would learn a lot more about the human body and mind. I believe dualism is all around us, especially in nature. Don't just see; look, and you will see more.

THE ETERNAL VORTEX, God is the consciousness of the universe.

Chapter 8: Mediumship

Carl Gustav Jung, a famous psychologist, has suggested that most dualism is rooted in an unhealthy separation of the psyche, such as that of the ego from a deeper self, resulting imbalance of total harmony. However, it could be argued that the resultant `tension` may be helpful to creative effort. Certainly, where mediumship is concerned, the polarity seems to be essential, but nevertheless, we should be aware of the negative aspects which may arise, thus maintaining a harmonious interchange of dualism and permitting positive enfoldment of the mediumistic potential.

Everyone who has taken part in ballroom dancing will understand the interchange of energy between the male and female polarity. When harmony is achieved between the participants, an interchange of energy takes place, and in the words of the song, `I could have danced all night`. However, when harmony is not achieved, look out for depletion of energy and aching feet!

Ignorance of this law may lead to a serious degeneration of the personality, the effects of which are only too obvious. A spirit medium unable to make the necessary harmonious interchange and compensation at a spiritual level may find that the subjective polarity becomes dominant in a negative sense, leading to a breakdown of the development process, a situation which can lead to seeking compensation through strong drink, drug, etc., or other escapist avenues.

The young medium should be aware that numerous aspirants have risen quickly in public acclaim only to fade away more quickly. (**The applause of the populace is soon spent; the applause of the unseen hosts lasts forever**).

Many are unable to cope with the crisis which comes from the separation or polarising of the psyche in the normal process of mediumistic development. The desire for public acclaim and over flamboyant personalities are often indicative of the imbalanced medium. It is not my purpose to attack these victims of ignorance but rather to suggest methods that could lead towards the realisation of greater potential. These critical periods of development have been recognised in the past and were referred to as `testing times`.

It is apparent that children are not encouraged to sit in the development circle, and I feel this to be a fundamental error. The child who exhibits signs of mediumship must be provided with the facilities to unfold. Spiritualist teaching states that the child is the repository of infinite possibility, but how can we evoke these possibilities when the flowering of them is discouraged? Once the portal has become obscured with more worldly pursuits, the development process becomes proportionately more difficult. Years are spent by people in later life trying to regain their psychic potential, which was evident in their pre-adolescent period, a point beautifully expressed by Thomas Treharne, poet and mystic.

When he wrote:

"The heaven was an oracle and spake divinity.

The earth did undertake the office of priest.

And I being dumb (nothing beside was dumb)

All things did come with voices and instruction.

But when I had gained a tongue, their power began to die.

Mine ears let other noises in, not theirs."

We must take a note from the foregoing that psychic potential can be vanquished at puberty, or conversely, maybe activated, e.g., `Poltergeist phenomena. The problem is seemingly that of a psychological balance, which affects the accessibility of the subconscious mind in either a negative or positive manner. It is important that consciousness should be expanded. We need to live in the larger context of understanding which psychic faculties permit. I suspect that an individual can only reach full maturity when his consciousness is expanded. A man with psychic gifts, if his faculties are reliable and if he is free of self-interest, can help his fellows in ways no other can help. Anyone who wants to train for psychic development must approach their task with an unclouded ego and be free from all selfishness jealousy. An open mind is also important, but an open nature is more important; this is the clarity the saints speak of, and the scientist knows, at least in relation to his work. You need to start with the truth in action, speech, and attitude. A lie detector registers untruth because the psychophysical mechanism registers deviation, but a student does not always know, consciously, when he has departed from the truth.

In any walk of life, the ability to discern truth is rare, and the ability to speak the truth is even rarer. In psychic work, this careful handling of truth is a necessity if one ever expects to have an open vision. One asks, "How can I maintain this perception of Honesty", It would be a challenge indeed to try to fight for that perception of reality throughout eternity. When one hears the voice of truth within them, the ego will be less.

Eventually, only God's voice is heard. That is when True Knowledge exists rather than perception.

It takes only one instance to prove that consciousness operates free of the body. For scientific observation, one instance may be of interest, but for practical purposes, expanded consciousness needs to be reproducible, reliable, and amenable to direction. It is my experience that expansion of consciousness can be developed. In other words, those psychic faculties can be induced and trained. My spasmodic psychic faculties were trained. Perhaps disciplined is a better word. Moreover, there are rules for this discipline. Some of them I stumbled upon, although they have been known for thousands of years; some were taught to me. There is nothing original about them. They are the laws that operate any time, any place. They may be phrased variously to suit different cultures but however stated they produce results when followed. It is important that consciousness should be expanded. The race needs to live in the larger context of understanding which psychic faculties permit.

The student will find themselves altering their daily habits. In the western world, we find our sleep patterns are irregular. As a result, we must catch up on our sleep. We need at least eight hours of undisturbed sleep to repair and build up our energies. The organs of the physical body must work together rhythmically, which will create the harmonisation of the auric field and our electromagnetic field. The student needs to look at their nourishment; if this is not mentioned by the teacher, then the alert student will discover that what they eat does make the difference. A balanced diet with the right number of vitamins provides the right substances for creating energy, which is vital for spirit communication. The student will find tobacco clouds the sensitivity, and alcohol does not help psychic development. If you do use these two substances, your psychic powers will be limited. We all must face up to the fact of character implications of psychic training.

You may ignore these; remember the test comes back and back until they are met, and then we move to the next level of spirit communication and spiritual knowledge.

The student will find their emotional level will change also. You will find being angry, anxious or being in a negative state will affect your breathing. We need to keep our breathing in a rhythmically way, and any of these negative habits will hinder our progress. The student will find themselves avoiding all negative energies even the small undesirable situation would put the student off balance, and this will slow or stop the psychic progression.

The student starts to understand the Laws of Nature and becomes, let's say, "in touch with nature" and begins to understand that all life forms play an important role in the workings of the earth. The student has to respect all creatures and the environment, they become oneness with all living forms of life, and they will then start to understand the laws of nature. It is vital that every student understands the laws of nature, and they must try to abide by them. All students will have to face up to their own conscious minds. They will find that when they have learnt to relax, their mind starts to wander, and everyday thoughts enter the mind. This is what we term the "clearing out phase" each thought should be analysed, do not try to reject these thoughts; they are part of the training.

The student will find if they are accepted by the spiritual teachers, if they are suitable for further development of their psychic powers, you must learn how to relax the mind and place unconditional trust into spiritual teachings. They will select the best method of teaching that would be of benefit for you and what type of communication is suitable. Sometimes you might not receive what you want, and not everybody is suitable for a particular part of development. Always be grateful, accept what you have and progress again. There could be changes as you develop. They will choose you, only if they can work with you. There are no special techniques other than patience, trust, and confidence. You must prepare yourself and be committed, and do your research about the psychic world and the different ways of communication.

I suggest reading books in the earlier years of 1830 – 1960; they are very informative books that will help you and explain in detail about spirits and the many ways of psychic phenomenon. You should be able to purchase some of these books in any good bookshop. Research the physical body, physics, and scientific investigations. Study the universe, the stars, and understand the earth, energies, and atoms of the earth. Spirits teacher can only use the word content that's in your mind. The more knowledge you gain, the more spirits can impress your mind.

Don't just leave it to the spirit teachers; we must have spiritual knowledge and an open mind, above all an understanding of the different ways in which spirits are able to communicate with you. You may find that your spirit teachers might not want you to become a medium; they may feel you have a special energy to become a healer or lecturer. In the earlier stages of development, don't be disappointed if you find yourself doing something different from what you desired. You are still working for spirit regardless of what they teach you, be happy. They know what is best suited for you.

You cannot force yourself to work as a medium if your energy is directed toward healing. You will find that during your time working for the spirit, they might change your direction to some other method of energy. Working for spirit also brings its rewards in the form of feelings, in the way of contentment, and you will find that you are at peace with yourself. You will begin to realise that the world is a school of learning, and we must go through good and bad experiences in life. We learn and pass on our knowledge to our children, and they will do the same. You will find yourself dealing with life situations with a calmer outlook, and you will realise what matters most is your life and not your life situations.

Once you have decided to develop your psychic senses, you have to be totally committed, and nothing should be allowed to hinder you. You need to sit quietly for spirit at the same time at least twice a week for a time of forty minutes, no more than one hour. It is best to sit when you know that you will not be disturbed or distracted. However, if you cannot find time to sit quietly for a period due to family commitments or other situations, then I would advise you to seek a psychic centre and no doubt they will have likeminded people who want to develop their psychic powers and am sure they will have a developing class.

A development class would be of benefit for you because the group energy would be stronger, and this could help you to develop at a steady pace, and you would be able to share your psychic experiences, and you will receive feedback that would encourage you further in your development. However, before you rush out to find a developing class, there are a few things you should consider, they are as follows.

- An experienced development class teacher. (How many years working)
- How many are in the class (four to eight members)
- There should be equal females and males.
- What room is the development class used. (Noise, distractions, not used)
- Other students (easy to get on with)
- Trust, honesty respect for one another
- Safety, precautions exist
- Second in command.
- Spiritual book, information
- Confidentiality

I cannot stress enough the development class teacher should be a person with many years of experience as a working medium (demonstrating). They should also have a wealth of knowledge regarding the enfoldment of psychic potential. All students need to rely on your development teacher to explain any uncertainness or any spiritual teachings they do not understand. You will experience energies around you, smells and different spirits will draw close, and if you are not sure of anything or felt uncomfortable in your meditation, your development class teacher can guide you and explain your experiences. It is also vital that you listen to your development teacher and if there is anything that you do not understand, then ask. It does not matter how silly the question might seem; you are there to learn. Your development teacher will know when the time is right for a public demonstration, which will be in a few years at least. Do not demonstrate in public or private readings unless your development teacher says you are ready.

The aspiring medium should be aware that numerous aspirants have demonstrated to the public before finishing their development only to find themselves in an embarrassing situation. I have been made aware that some spirit mediums have been demonstrating clairvoyance to the public after sitting in a development class for a period of only two months and opening psychic shops. This is absurd; these people only do more damage than good. I would never encourage a student to go public until they have gained sufficient spiritual experience. They would need to be introduced to the stage or a spiritualist church platform by their respective development teacher. Don't expect to develop your psychic sense within a period of six months. If that is your goal, then I am sorry to disappoint you. Your development can be from two years to five years at least. As I said, this is a lifetime commitment, and you really need to be dedicated. It is often said that when the student is ready, the spirit teacher appears. When I was ready, the spirit guide knew when this would be, the spirit teacher appeared. However, before you demonstrate publicly, your development teacher will let you accompany them on a spiritualist church platform or stage for the first few months to let you gain some experience. Now you see why I have said your development teacher needs many years' experience in demonstrating.

Public speaking can be very daunting at the best of times. This can make you freeze and panic when you are standing on stage or platform for the first time. Knowing that everyone is waiting to hear your voice, your development teacher will take some of the pressure off you. You will gradually build your confidence and gain some experience which will help you. You will have to learn how to relax the mind and body to allow the communion of spirit helpers to impress their thoughts onto your mind. Everyone has nerves before they start their demonstration. You would not be normal if you didn't have nerves. I have conducted many clairvoyance demonstrations, and still, I get that sickly feeling in the pit of my stomach. If this really bothers you, then you need to practise with small groups or any opportunity that comes along to demonstrate your psychic powers. For a year, I visited spiritualist churches and attended their open circle service. An open circle is where like-minded people can practise their psychic powers to the group. I found this to be an excellent way of gaining experience, confidence, and encouragement to demonstrate off stage. You are not like an entertainer who has a script to follow, and it takes a tremendous amount of confidence knowing you must totally rely on your inner self and the communion of spirit helpers. Spirits will not let you down, trust them, and they will trust you. Your spirit helpers are aware you are about to work on their behalf. Why would they let you down? They won't! Trust them!

Everyone is a combination of energies in moving patterns, which influences every other individual who shares the same field of force. A certain quantum of energy is constantly exchanged between individuals.

For example, a person (A) and person (B) exchange a definite charge of energy. The amount varies in accordance with the intensity and the frequency levels of contact. This exchange of energy affects the permanent channel of communication. The channel having once been opened interchange is possible between those two individuals, whether both are living or one of them discarnate. A third person (C), who has had contact with both (A) and (B) at one stage, can relay from one to the other but cannot make direct contact with (A) and (B). This crisscross of ``wires'' of energy binds them to many people, maybe thousands of people. Person (C) no doubt has met many people in daily life when they were in the physical body, and some of them would have moved to the discarnate state. However, the ties persist. Another example: If Jacqueline Higgins touched her great-grandfather when he was in the physical body, they remain in touch, and direct contact persists.

If Jacqueline never knew her great grandfather, she would have to get someone like her grandfather, who knew them both, to communicate, which is only possible if both Jacqueline and her great grandfather wanted to communicate.

Remember, this is a lifetime commitment!

The priority is to emphasise that mediumship is a spiritual function and to dispel certain `modern` concepts which state that there is no connection between spiritual awareness and mediumship. I state categorically that attention to spiritual enfoldment is vital to the proper development of mediumship. Perhaps there is confusion between ordinary psychic or E.S.P. phenomena and mediumship: the latter requires a communicating spirit, whereas the former does not. Unfortunately, many psychic demonstrations are passed off as mediumship, all too often accompanied by various `gimmicks`. In mediumship, there is a shift in consciousness by which the etheric senses are activated and their impulses registered in the medium's mind. It is essential, therefore, that the psychological balance should be strong, and anymore suffering from mental weakness would be well advised to seek authoritative medical advice before proceeding. The essential factor is to develop and strengthen the spiritual nature, thereby permitting the necessary harmonious interchange to take place within the human polarities. Yogis have long understood this problem.

Andrew Jackson Davis has the following excellent advice to offer.

In the morning arise resolved to do nothing against, but everything for, the Kingdom of heaven on earth.

Happiness being the object, let every action during the day be preceded by such well-conceived and well-developed thoughts as tending to its attainment.

At night retire at peace with yourself, at peace with the entire world.

Draw these axioms into your soul. I know them to be the first steps towards happiness and culture. If you fail to take these properly, quietness and development are beyond your attainment. See well to this admonition. It is the language of no theory; it's the voice of truth.

The law and method of spiritual culture also require the following direction:

Be contented with the past and with all it has brought you.

Be thankful for the present and all you have

Be patient for the future and for all it promises to bring you.

Next, consider the outward means of spiritual culture.

Study the exact or physical sciences, the laws of the body and the law of the spirit. Indulge in proper gratification of the external senses, walking, playing, dancing, and various amusements, reading, writing essays, keeping journals, and associating with good and ornamentally educated minds. This includes all things that have to do with practising self-discipline and obeying the principle of wisdom.

Concerning the outward means of spiritual culture, let me remark:

By studying the sciences, I mean those sciences which relate to the organisation. The science anatomy of physiology, chemistry, and reproduction.

The study of physical and mental laws has intended the principles of anatomical motion of physiological functions and measurement of power and the principles of mental action and predisposition. These sciences and laws should be studied. The infant should be instructed according to their decisions, and parents should be qualified to impart this instruction. I feel no child should be sent to school before the child has attained an age of eight years and generally not before its tenth year. I feel premature education is burdensome and paralysing to the faculties and passions. Precocious youths are seldom strong and powerful men. They spring into life and leave it before the period in which the natural mind is allowed to develop and mature.

A proper gratification of the senses is intended whatever the preceding sciences and principles will teach and permit as essential to health and cultivation. What is said further of the outward means is applicable to children, students and every individual who desires harmony in body and in mind.

From this proceed to the inward means of spiritual culture, which are.

Self-analysis, self-discipline, self-confession of faults and self-harmonisation.

Studying spiritual or psychological sciences, the sciences of analogy and picturesque geography.

Studying paintings and music, Meditation, Poetical contemplation, Conversations

Mutual assistance and mutual manipulations of spirit communion with higher spheres of spiritual life.

The value of self-analysis or introspection is apparent to all.

To gain an understanding of self, it is necessary to look inward and examine the contents of your mind and the general makeup of your character. Not one of us is without faults, but we are often unconscious of them simply because we do not try to analyse our character. This process calls for uncompromising honesty, and we shall find that however many others may be disposed to look with charitable eyes upon us, we shall be stern enough in our judgement upon our own mental makeup. This is the first step towards rounding out whatever angularities of character may be ours. The value of the other rules is obvious. Of the last communion with the higher spheres of life, what is meant by such communication is something more than a casual conversation we have with our spirit friends in séance. That has its value, but real spirit communication is a lifting of the mind to a higher plane of life, an aspiration of the soul that is met with a corresponding inspiration.

It enriches the mind, deepens the emotional nature, broadens the understanding, and brings a great peace such we cannot find in our life every day. It strengthens, refreshes, and tones the mind, creating a love for all that is beautiful, true, and good. Such communication can be entered into at any time and in any place when we truly desire it. Often, we shall find companionship when there are no earthly friends nearby. Nature then becomes a source of inspiration and strength, for we commune with her and through her with our father, God. It requires but little time to learn what is useful, to learn what is just, to learn what is power and beauty. Aspiration and harmony are familiarly explained in the fields of universal nature and humanity. A harmonious individual is a revelation of the Divine Mind. The science, the chemistry and mechanism of Divine Creation are represented in the human form, and the holy elements and attributes of God are incarnated in every human spirit. To be like heaven let us aspire to heaven; to be like God, let us aspire to God.

Harmony must begin with the individual. It will thence spread over families, societies and nations, and then the whole world will represent the individual, and the individual will represent the whole. And God will be all in all.

DO NOT DISMISS THESE RULES BECAUSE OF THE SIMPLICITY

Great truths are hidden from the wise.

Chapter 9: Preparing for a Demonstration of Mediumship

During the day, we collect all types of unwanted energies and smells that linger on our clothes and in our aura (electromagnetic field). We get used to the smells of pollution and different odours. Even our perfumes become part of us. Family or friends are always willing to tell you about the bad situations they have found themselves in or about a disagreement they have had with someone. You listen to their complaints, which is a form of negative energy. These are just some of the reasons why you should prepare yourself before working on behalf of the spirit world. It is difficult for spirit communicators to convey messages, and we should try to limit all obstructions where possible. Any good medium will tell you how difficult it is trying to create the link between the two worlds. I feel it is vital that you prepare yourself, and you will find that all good mediums have their own way of preparing themselves. If you do not prepare yourself for work, how can you work for spirit to the best of your ability? Preparing for the spirit gives you that psychological advantage knowing that you are ready for work.

When I am working on behalf of the spirit world, I always prepare myself, so I can give them the best channel for communication without any extra physical difficulties where possible. It's extremely difficult for spirit to communicate with you at the best of times, so why make it harder. What you can do is prepare yourself in a way to provide the best links. When I am ready and prepared, I have found myself refreshed, confident and have the sense of excitement, knowing spirits are aware? I am ready for work in the sacred office of Mediumship which is a lifetime commitment. If you do not prepare yourself for the spirit helpers, by relaxing the mind and cleansing the body of all odours, you will find it difficult to recognise; let's say a smell! The spirit communicators are trying to make you aware of, or if your mind is still thinking about the day's events, this will only hinder communications between the spirit helpers and yourself resulting in bad communication, or you could miss some important evidence for the recipient. It is very important that you prepare yourself. Just like your spirit helpers, they will be prepared in the spirit world.

Always remember this is a team effort, and there is no `I` in a team.

I follow this procedure whenever I am demonstrating clairvoyance in public, whether on stage or for a private reading. It will give you some idea of how to prepare, and you will establish what's the best format is for you. Remember though! It's important to be in the right frame of mind, "Passive Mind"; that's what your aim is.

Three hours before the demonstration of Mediumship start to prepare in the following way;

1. Find somewhere where you can sit quietly and relax, I sit on the bed with the curtains drawn and the door closed. Fixed your eyes on an object like a picture; this will help to relax your mind.

2. Let the day's thoughts enter your mind, analyse them individually, do not fight these thoughts, except and let them go. You're mentally clearing the mind.

3. Start to visualise your demonstration; the building, people, layout, seating, music and how you will conduct yourself. This is your kind of rehearsal before the live performance. Your aim is to build a mental picture in your mind.

4. You do not need to worry about your spirit helpers. They will be preparing as well.

5. Send your thoughts to the spirit world, asking for the highest of communication with the divine spirit.

6. Two hours before the demonstration, have a light meal; sandwich, salad, energy drink or water. Food that's easy digested and does not lie on the stomach. Drink plenty of water to clear the toxins from the body.

7. Have a shower or bath to cleanse the physical body of all smells, including perfumes. Use non-scented soap to remove all the odours. If in a shower, stand for a few

minutes to rinse the body and visualise the water taking away all negative thoughts. Take deep breaths and visualise freshness and positive energy.

8. After the shower, do not put any perfumes on. We do not want anything to interfere with spirit smells.

9. Your clothing must be comfortable but smart. The first impression is very important; this will make the audience relax. No aftershaves or perfumes to be worn.

10. Meditate for thirty minutes, closing your eyes and mentally saying a prayer, thanking the spirit world for the day's events. Say to spirit, "when the demonstration starts, your physical body is in their hands, every word you say or every action you make, you know it's from spirit". Then totally relax and enjoy the stillness of your body and mind.

11. I do not again think about the demonstration until upon arrival. I put it to the back of my mind, knowing I am prepared and will be ready for work.

12. You will need, if possible, a driver to take you to the venue to avoid any unfortunate circumstances. However, if you cannot find a driver, you will need to have a clear mind when driving to your venue, therefore leave in plenty of time and arrive there at least thirty minutes before start time. Any adjustments can be addressed, and again you can have a quiet time to relax before you start your demonstration.

These twelve points are my Golden Rules! Simple as they are, but very important. I find when I start to prepare, my spirit helpers are preparing as well. I would suggest you use these Golden Rules when you have decided; a medium is what you want to be. I used these rules throughout my time in the developing class and still do today. You are still working for the spirit during your development stage; therefore, I am advising you to start preparing yourself from the beginning, and after a time, it will become part of you. If you have any other methods of preparing and you feel that way is best suited for you, then stick with it and don't give up. You have a GIFT from the spirits. Treat it as a gift, don't abuse your gift or use your gift against others; mind you, spirits will not let you! Just because you have been given a gift does not mean you are above the laws of nature. You are not! Everybody needs to prepare. It's like putting the icing on the cake. You must be dedicated to your true beliefs. You will find your psychic gift will become stronger, and your spirit helpers will know how committed you are. After your developing stages, and you feel you are ready to work as a spirit medium, don't have the attitude you're learning, or teaching has ceased, they have not. You will continuously be learning because energies are changing all the time. This is a life commitment, whereby each day, you will progress. Some people view psychics as a career, and why not. But never abuse your spiritual or psychic gift. Knowledge for the benefit of mankind. Your remarkable psychic powers can be of help to humanity and the future of this planet.

Chapter 10: Mental Mediumship

Mental Mediumship is used mainly by today's mediums in the form of telepathy between the medium and spirit helpers. Mental Mediumship, as the term suggests, relies upon the mind or mental processes for the purposes of communication with spirit communicators. It may only be the individual spirit medium of who is aware of the communication. The main types of mental Mediumship include clairvoyance (seeing), clairaudience (hear), and clairsentience (feel, sense). All mediums possess a combination of these three forms. In spirit communication, the spirit helper brings the spirit entity into contact with the person on earth. Between the medium and spirit helper, a close harmonious partnership exists, thus providing the line of communication between the two worlds. The spirit helper can blend with the medium's mind so that thoughts are submitted from the spirit world, which is in turn translated by the medium into descriptions of places or people and in words of a message, through clairvoyance, clairaudience or clairsentience.

We will look at each of the different forms or types of spiritual Mediumship below:

Clairvoyance

In the case of clairvoyance, the medium receives images as the means of communication. These may be images in the mind's eye of the medium, or less frequently, the medium may see a spirit person or object as if they are viewing them with their physical eye. In the latter case, it is possible that the spirit is connecting with the visual mechanism within the medium's brain rather than the source of the image being in the actual external environment. The images that we see of people and objects in the everyday world are a construction of the brain. But the spirit person will appear to the medium as if they are in the external environment. However, this explanation is speculative. No one is likely to be able to come to a definitive answer to this in the near future. For whatever reasons, spirit communications about the precise details of the mechanisms of Mediumship can at times be vague or conflicting.

In the case of other images, the medium will, of necessity, be more actively involved in their interpretation. Preferably they can relay the image to the person who they think is the recipient of the communication, and the person may be able to interpret the image for themselves. However, it is likely that the spirit medium will become more involved at some point, and this interpretation of the meaning of images can give rise to many difficulties. It is particularly so in the case of symbols. Some have a commonly held meaning, but many can be interpreted in different ways influenced by the experiences and memories of each individual person. Our own spirit teachers tell us that spirits experiment with using symbols with spirit mediums to see how they interpret them in order that they can then refine the process of communication. However, at times they may give a symbol aimed more at the recipient's manner of interpretation than the mediums. As with all forms of Mediumship, it is a transaction or interaction between at least three parties. The process of communication at times may have more the feel of a game of charades rather than a clear dialogue. Images can also be used to facilitate the process. For example, some spirit mediums may see the light or words or some other sign above or to the side of the intended recipient to facilitate the identification of the person to whom the message is intended.

Clairaudience

With clairaudience, the spirit medium hears voices or other sounds, and this is the means of communication. As with clairvoyance, the medium may hear the sounds either within their mind or as if with their physical ear. When sounds such as music and other noises occur, there can again be issues around interpretation in a similar way to clairvoyance. Sounds or a voice can come very quickly to the spirit medium; therefore, it is essential there is no disturbance from the audience. Clairaudience is believed to be the ability to hear sounds beyond the normal hearing range in a spiritual sense.

Clairaudient messages sound like someone talking in your mind. It will never be tormenting. The tone will be the same as always: even and calm. You may think you have heard by your physical ear. Actually, you hear these sounds, voices, noises within the mind, the etheric body.

Clairsentience

A spirit medium that works through clairsentience senses a spirit's presence. This may occur in a variety of ways: general sensing of a presence, sensing an emotion, changes in temperature, breezes, a feeling of cobwebs on the face, a smell, scent, or fragrance. The vagueness of some of these impressions can make the process more difficult. However, sensing that a person's grandmother is present along with an awareness of the favourite scent which she used to use can be very evidential. Most spirit mediums start off with clairsentience, and some never progress further. However, don't be fooled into thinking clairsentient is the weaker of spirit communication; it is not, there has been some remarkable evidence conveyed. You will never know which form of communication you will be used for demonstrations.

You could use clairvoyance, and then next time, you could use another type of form. I often hear spirit mediums say, "I am clairvoyance, or I am clairaudient" don't be like one of these types of people. You're a mental medium. Be happy with that; who knows later, you could develop Physical Mediumship, which is another in-depth spirit communication which would completely confuse you at this stage. As my spirit teachers and earth teachers keep on telling me; take your time, be patient, it's not a race, all good things come to those you wait and be patient. A mental medium still finds it difficult sometimes to relay reliable messages to the recipient due to many obstacles. I always seek knowledge of recent events from spirit helpers, meaning something the recipient did or they can relate to within the last few days. This, without a doubt, proves eternal life, and you are communicating with spirit.

In mental or subjective Mediumship, there is a quickening of the mental aura. The colour radiations appear to become more intense, and this aspect has been widely reported by clairvoyants. In earlier writings, this has been referred to as a cap or funnel observed upon the medium's head. In my own observations, this has always been represented by powerful golden radiation within the mental aura, seen not only in subjective phases of Mediumship but also very markedly in good inspirational speakers.

Undoubtedly the aura plays an extremely important role in Mediumship, and all aspiring mediums should pay particular attention to this matter. In the past spiritual development has been described as 'building a rainbow bridge', in other words living one's life in such a way that the refined colour tones of spiritual evolution are demonstrated in the aura. The spirit medium is part of the sacred office, which demands a hundred per cent commitment. The modern approach, held fortunately by a few, to divorce the development of Mediumship from its spiritual implications, reveal an astonishing degree of ignorance where basic knowledge of the mechanics of Mediumship is concerned.

Spiritual Laws cannot be ignored, and the progressive phases of Mediumship require proper unfoldment within the aura; of this, the student will be assured.

In psychometry, where the radiations from an object are analysed, the connection with the aura is obvious. Through the auric atmosphere, the psychometrist can 'feel' or probe the atmosphere of the object under investigation. Development depends upon the ability to recognise the intrusion of 'foreign' vibrations and the degree of accuracy obtained in their interpretation.

Much has been said about the apparent ability of some mediums to command a flow of mediumistic phenomena often compared with water running from a tap. Genuine Mediumship is subject to an ebb and flows consistent with the depletion and restoration of auric vitality. Dowsers in the field have long been aware of sudden magnetic reversals and polarising effects, which all too often have necessitated the postponement of work until such time as the radiesthesia images reappear. I believe that it is extremely probable that similar conditions arise in the human aura from time to time, during which mediumistic sensitivity is adversely affected. This is particularly emphasised during electrical storms, when Mediumship is quite definitely prone to interference, as also is dowsing.

During demonstrations of subjective Mediumship, the consciousness of the medium is raised to the level of the etheric senses. It is with the etheric senses that spirit visitors are registered and not with the physical, sensory organs. The increased vitality of the mental aura during mediumistic activity extends to the etheric aura, although it is not so easily observed. It is due to this apparent vital charging that communication takes place, and the simple shift from physical to etheric consciousness may be the cause of the auric effect described. In this connection, however, it must be remembered that consciousness itself remains something of a mystery. Truly there is much to learn in our pursuit of spiritual knowledge.

Chapter 11: Public Speaking

The serious student would have spent considerable time in the development circle ranging from two years to five years or even more. Some students may be guided to demonstrate their spiritual skills to the public, whether it may be on the platform of a Spiritualist Church or on a Public Stage. Spirit mediums play a vital role in spiritualism by proving evidence of eternal life by way of spirit communication. Spirit Mediums should have extensive knowledge of the phenomena of spiritualism and philosophy. Sometimes mediums can select the wrong recipient for which a message is to be passed on, and this can be indicated by the recipient not understanding the message, therefore, breaking the link and offering the message to the audience. I am sure the spirit message will be correct, and it's usually the medium that gets it wrong. Some people will say yes just for you to speak to them and will take everything you say to them. As you gain experience will be able to identify those kinds of people. Always maintain the truth and be honest to yourself and to those around you.

Never let your ego take over when you are demonstrating clairvoyance, which can easily happen. The ego is part of the physical body and not part of your spirit body; therefore, if you become flamboyant or have a cocky attitude, you are not working with spirits. It takes a lot of resilience to subdue your ego, especially when people complain to you for your work. Always keep grounded, and your psychic gift will always be of a high standard. Any bad taste or colourful language should NEVER be used when representing spirits' energies. They will not allow colourful language in their messages or indicate anything bad for the recipient. If this happens, it is the brain of the spirit medium and not the spirit mind.

You are always in control, and common sense should be used; spirits cannot force anything on you against your will at any time.

I have witnessed people who claim to be spirit mediums or psychics using colourful language when passing messages from the spirit energies. Also, I have heard them mention bad messages from the spirit communicator, which scared the recipient. It is the mind of the charlatan, not the spirit communicator. This is totally unacceptable, and spirit mediums/psychics who are guilty of this are insufficiently developed. It is important for you to understand you are providing evidence of eternal life beyond our physical death, which gives substance to the teachings of spiritualism. You should never place a recipient in an embarrassing situation by a personal remark or harassing them. Many newcomers to spiritualism have been known to turn their backs on spiritual topics after being bullied or dictated to. A spirit medium who conducts themselves in this unruly manner should stop practising Mediumship and seek the advice of an experience spirit medium, who in turn would be more than willing to help.

It is necessary to crawl before attempting to walk. Practising in public speaking should be undertaken as often as possible. There are many venues open to the trainee spirit medium/psychic to practise his/her speaking skills. The time will come when you want to demonstrate your skills in public, and believe me. This is not easy. A good development class teacher will let you accompany them on the platform or stage when they are demonstrating clairvoyance. This would provide you with valuable experience, and you will realise this is another level of your training. Your development teacher will give you the opportunity to offer your message from spirit to the audience, and she/he will assess you and guide you if you have any difficulties with your message. You will find some people who are sceptical and often than not you are guided to them. I believe this is a spiritual test; however, your teacher will help you, don't be afraid of asking for help; you are there to learn. This experience will help you to decide whether you want to demonstrate to the public. Do not feel you are letting spirits or your development teacher down; they will understand. It does not mean that you have failed;

there is no test at the end of your development stages. Some people can demonstrate to the public by providing some wonderful evidence from spirit to the recipient. Working off a platform, or a stage, even in a spiritual centre, is not easy, and if you struggle after a few attempts, do not worry. When the time is right and you want to demonstrate to the public, it will happen.

I have known some wonderful people who have very strong links with the spirit world only to find it extremely hard to relax in front of a large crowd. It is important to remember that you have been given a spiritual gift to enjoy peace of mind. There are other avenues of spiritual work which you might find will suit you. There will be many options for you, so do not panic.

The students who want to pursue their Mediumship and demonstrate their psychic senses to the public need to look at Public Speaking. Yes, I know you will not have a script, and your information comes from the spirit communicator. Making speeches in public or giving professional presentations is not an easy task to do. You will feel the butterflies in your stomach, your legs feeling like jelly. Your mind becomes cluttered and confused, and your voice will speed up, and your words will come out all wrong. Your body will do all kinds of unpleasant things to you when you must stand up and look at the sea of faces with the view of getting the spirit communicators message across with the evidence and in a compelling, interesting way. Some students just think of getting off the platform or stage as quickly as possible as embarrassment overwhelms them.

I don't mean to scare you, just to remind you that your body reacts in extremis when put under pressure, and for most students, public speaking is just about the worst pressure they can be put under. It's normal to be nervous and have a lot of anxiety when speaking in public. In a way, it's not normal to have nerves or anxiety; in fact, everyone has nerves and anxiety about public speaking. Public speaking may not be comfortable, but take my word for it; nerves are good. Being on centre stage is not a good place to feel too comfortable; nerves will keep you awake and ensure you don't get too complacent.

Your audience can be your friend unless you know you're absolutely facing a hostile group of people. Human nature is such that your audience wants you to relax, and they're on your side. Therefore, rather than assuming they don't like you, give them the benefit of the doubt, and you will find yourself growing in confidence. They aren't an anonymous sea of faces but real people. So, to help you gain more confidence when speaking in public, think of ways to engage your audience. The one thing you don't want is for them to fall asleep! But make no mistake, some churches or arenas are designed to do just that: dim lights, cushy chairs, and sitting quietly, a perfect invitation to catch up on those knaps. There are several ways of maintaining the audience's attention. Maintain eye contact for a second or two with as many people as possible, change the pace of your delivery and the volume of your voice. If you make a mistake, that's fine. Recovering from your mistake makes you appear more human, and a good recovery puts your audience at ease. They will identify with you more. I always find humour helps you to build that initial relationship with the audience, especially at the beginning; gentle humour is good in place of jokes. There is nothing worse than a punch line that has no punch. It's worth telling them some personal experiences to bring the right atmosphere which will increase the energy for you.

When you are on a platform or stage, don't just stand in one place; move around. You will find the audience will follow every move you make. Now you have their attention. However, be careful with your mannerism; lose those bad habits, for example, holding a glass full of water, whistling. Yes, I have heard spirit mediums whistle as they are demonstrating. Use your body language to help you to convey your message.

The smart appearance will send out the right signals to your audience. Always make sure you have clean clothes pressed (yes, with an iron). When you walk on a platform or stage, look around the audience and smile. Let them be aware that you are looking forward to speaking to them by using your body language. Speak in a smooth tone and clear voice; project your voice so everyone can hear. I find it best to establish this at the beginning by asking those people at the back of the church or arena if they can hear.

Do not make someone in the audience uncomfortable because they will close on you, and this will, in turn, get the audience to feel sorry for them, which will lower the energy.

It is harder for a spirit medium to stand on stage than any other entertainer. If you were a presenter, you would have a script, or if you were a musician, then you would have songs. As a medium, you do not have anything, only trust with the spirit communicator that they are going to bring you're the links for conveying a message from them to the recipient, which will suggest eternal life. There have been many times when I have stood on a platform or stage and not been aware of my spirit guides until the last second, and that is usually when I select a person to create a link. You must have this trust and remain relaxed; don't let your nerves get the better of you. Follow the first thing that enters your mind, and once you have started, you will find your messages and links will flow naturally. The first link is always the most difficult of all.

You will gain experience and find your own way of working; you will develop your own routine that is best suited for you. Never, I repeat, never copy another spirit medium's style of demonstrating. It will only lead to disaster, and the audience will be aware you are emulating. If you are happy with your way of demonstrating, then stick with it, you will find the more you demonstrate in public, the better the demonstrations will be. I have my routine, and I am always looking to improve, never be complacent and take things for granted. You will soon trip up. Arrive at the church or arena in plenty of time; I would say at least thirty to forty minutes. This is the time you can unwind and relax and focus all your thoughts on the evening. You should never say that you are working with spirit. When you are not, do not give a message until you are sure that the message has come from the spirit helpers. I have seen spirit mediums say they are working with spirit, and they know that they are not. If you have not got a link at the start, inform the audience and talk about something that is related to you or about spiritualism. You could ask the audience if they have any questions about the psychic phenomenon. I bet you find a lot of hands go up. People always want their questions answered, and that is one of the reasons why you should gain spiritual knowledge by reading factual books written by old pioneers and scientific book that specialises in psychic phenomenon. If you cannot answer the questions, let them know you will find the answers and forward them to them. Never bluff the audience; they will suss you out. Sometimes you may have let the audience know there is no spirit comlink, which is not often. It is best, to be honest, and you will find the audience will have respect for you. I have on an occasion stated that I have no spirit link, and when I have conducted questions and answers, I always find I am ready for my first spirit message.

Even though you will be working for the spirit operators relaying messages, always be aware of your mannerism and how you conduct yourself on the platform or stage. Sloppiness produces poor performance.

You will be able to move with the energy of the audience, remember a lot of them have come to receive a message from their spirit loved ones. They will be sending out their thoughts to them even if they are not aware of this. The spirit operators will provide you with the right message and evidence for the recipient; it's the medium that sometimes gets it wrong. After all, we are only human, and humans do make mistakes. If you are providing a message to a recipient, and they say they don't understand or give you an acknowledgement of `No`, don't take it personally. They are not saying no to you; they mean they don't understand the message and the spirit operators will try again; you must always remain relaxed. There are many reasons why the recipient says `No`. They could be shy. Some people don't want to speak in the open about a situation or about their personal life. They could be timid sort of people. Sometimes when people say `No`, it's because they cannot think straight away of an incident or that family member or friend. Their mind goes blank, and you will find this happens often. Be aware the recipient, who received a message, and don't understand usually go home, and when they are relaxed, they remember their message and realise who connected with them. On many occasions when I have returned to the venue, people have told me they remembered their spirit communicator.

If you receive a `No from a recipient, never say you will ask for more evidence. Just stop and think! You have said that you have created a link with the spirit operator, who has provided you with a message to pass on to the recipient. So, what you are saying is that the spirits are with you, and they are aware of what's happening, so why do you need to ask. Don't you think the spirit operator knows what to do? Why waste energy? Wait until another message comes through. When you say to someone that you have a spirit standing near them, never ask if their mother or father or anyone else is in the spirit world. You should know you're the spirit medium! You should never ask if anybody is in the spirit world. As a matter of fact, you should never ask any questions. This will only put doubt in the mind of the recipient and the audience. It is important to have a three-way link, and that's means spirit, recipient, and you. This is what's needed to create a strong link. But remember, never ask for information from the recipient about a spirit family or friend. You provide the evidence; the recipient should confirm. It is ok to ask who the spirit person is. Sometimes you will find no matter what kind of spirit messages you pass on to a recipient. They will repeatedly say `No`. This is when you must admit you have got it wrong. The best way forward is to ask the audience if anyone understands; usually, you will find someone who can link to the message. If the audience does not understand, then pause, and try again with the recipient. However, don't spend too long trying to create a link as other members of the audience will get bored and fed up. If you have trust in your spirit helpers, you will have one thing less to worry about. The most important thing to do is learn to relax the mind and enjoy the demonstration. If you don't enjoy working on a platform or stage, then you should not be working in this manner.

- I have listed here some do and don'ts that will help you; these are guidelines only:
- DO's
- Ensure a practical working knowledge of spiritualism and physical and mental phenomenon.

- Selecting the right recipient for spirit messages.
- Give what is received without embellishment (give what you get).
- Monitor messages (try to keep track of your messages).
- Provide evidence of eternal life by descriptions, names, knowledge of recent events.
- Be always truthful and honest.
- Seek confirmation from the recipient about their message.
- Continue to sit for development, which is ongoing.
- Be smart and well-mannered.
- Ensure anything that needs to be researched at a later date.
- Always have respect for the recipient

DON`T

- Use colourful language or offensive remarks or embarrassment, dictatorship.
- Use personal remarks to the recipient or to family or friends.
- Bully a message on to a recipient or force a message on to them.
- Provide any medical diagnosis or about any medication.
- Add to the spiritual message or try to make the message fit the recipient

Change any message to suit the recipient.

Tell lies or make a message up for the recipient.

Predict the future or tell their fortune

Tell fairy stories (angels with wings or fantasy stories)

Use your common sense and always be respectful to the recipient, even if they are a sceptic. Demonstrating to the public can be rewarding and a sense of goodwill knowing that you have

worked hard and helped those who need help. However, you must remember you're not above the law of nature, and egoism plays no part in Mediumship.

Chapter 12: Third Eye (Known as the Mind's Eye)

It is very strange, but only in our harmonic determinism do we get the right conception of our responsibilities and are directed to the great mines of social wealth and power within ourselves. Consequently, we see how essential it is for us to have high and lofty conceptions of the capability for splendid service which lies within our human nature. Called the Third Eye in occult language, this `trigger` can release a vortex of psychic energy for the extension of awareness in new dimensions, for speeding up or slowing down time as experienced on our planet and achieving one hundred per cent personality integration.

Dr Douglas Baker reveals that the Third Eye derives its power from the pineal, pituitary, and parotid glands, allied to `whirlwinds` of energy known as `chakras` or force centres. There are seven of these centres in the human body. Their physical location is the base of the spine, the solar plexus, the spleen, the heart, the throat, the brow, and the top of the head.

Let's look at exercising the eye muscles and relieving tension in the area. These exercises are a necessary preliminary to turning the eyes inwards and upwards in the stages of meditation. Only the eyes move; do not move the head.

PLEASE DO NOT ATTEMPT any of the techniques hereinafter described without preparing your eye muscle in advance. For a full week, night, and morning, exercise your eyes muscles by gazing strongly at the extremes of the sockets. Safe methods are indicated in the exercise:

Move eyes to the extreme top of the sockets

Roll eyes to the extreme right and hold one second

Roll eyes to the extreme bottom and hold one second

Roll eyes to the extreme left and hold one second

Repeat these exercises at least ten times clockwise and ten times anti-clockwise.

The Finger Exercise

The two forefingers are held upright and extended. They should be placed at (comfortable) arm's length away from the eyes. They should be about six inches apart or may be spaced by the thumbs held at right angles to them. Concentrate on the space equidistant between the fingers and draw them together to make one finger. Practice this, and then see if you can visualise the third finger without the help of the other two. Energy follows thought, this is a basic principle of occult development, and in these exercises, the energy of high quality is directed to the region in front of the forehead.

Candles

Later, candles may be substituted for fingers. The candle flame seen as the third image has esoteric implications. It is said that 'where the blue meets the gold' the Third Eye may be found. Seeing the 'third' flame is good practice for visualising the similar structure of the Third Eye, which has often been described as flame-like.

The Coloured Cube

A cube of ten centimetres should be arranged so that each face is of a different colour. The colours should be the classical seven of the rainbows. The six used on the faces should be Red, Orange, Yellow, Green, Blue, and Violet. These may be placed randomly. The seventh colour, Indigo, has special significance and is used later. The cube faces should be studied separately. Intense concentration on each face should be a preliminary to visualising the colour on the opposite face. Then, the cube should be placed so that two sides can be seen at once and later, their opposite two faces visualised. Finally, the three faces of a cube should be studied, and then their opposite visualised. The last exercise then should be the visualisation of all the colours at once, seen as an indigo cube. Indigo is the colour of the solar logos and synthesises all others.

New Dimensions

The ability to think, perceive and act in new dimensions strengthens the formation of the Third Eye lens. The Third Eye is a four-dimensional organ and therefore flourishes in a situation in which control of time has become a developed capacity. Any sort of slowing down of time will enable the activity of the Third Eye to become more facile. The four dimensions are…. **LENGTH x BREADTH x HEIGHT x TIME**

A study of the writing of P .D Ouspensky's "A new Model of the Universe, and Rodney Collins, The Theory of Celestial Influence, will reward the student interested in New Dimensions. One may live a lifetime of experiences in a few seconds. On the other hand, as we have seen from Priestly experience of the birds on God's hill, time may be speeded up. This is how the real initiations of an aspirant are accomplished. It may take only a few seconds or a few minutes as the rod of initiation is applied but crowed into them are the rewards of lifetimes of experience.

Seeking the Third Eye of Others

In a way you have now been shown, gaze at the eyes of someone with whom you are in complete harmony. Try to see a third eye between the two. If the breath is used in conjunction with the synchronising act of focus, then great power over the one gazed at is soon developed. The ability to focus on minute locations in space should enable you to see specks of dust floating in the air. It was by this method that I began to see vitality globules. A little later, I was able to see them without much need for focus.

Crystal Gazing

There is a whole science of crystal gazing, but few understand how the process works. The clearest crystal can act as a concentration point for the lens being built out of ATMA-BUDDHI-MANAS. Perhaps this would be better understood if I were to relate an experience I had soon after beginning to wear spectacles for the first time (at about the age of 45). During self-hypnosis, when my consciousness had been placed in the inner vehicles poised just above the physical and when I can very frequently see the ceiling through my closed eyelids. I noticed that, despite the fact I was not wearing spectacles, the lens of the spectacles could be seen. In other words, wearing a lens of some sort constantly in front of the eyes had created a lens in higher

101

material. Thus, persistent gazing at a very pure lens or crystal helps attract material of subtler planes to simulate the same shape and clarity. It's necessary for a very clear and perfect spherical crystal to use. All the exercises described above have their applications to crystal gazing and should be repeated using a crystal wherever possible.

Chapter 13: Paranormal Activities Explained

We are forever reminded by the media and the film industry there are evil spirits, and they want to harm us or even possess our physical bodies. You have probably heard or seen films such as; Poltergeist, Ghosts, Zombies, and many other undesirable names. All these fictitious films are best left to the imaginary minds of the filmmakers or the media presenters. They play no part in spiritualism which is the seeker of the truth, just like science. I have met many people who have claimed to be possessed, or their house is haunted by evil spirits, and I have heard all types of unexplained stories. However, I have an open mind about these claims and will always try to help those people who claim to be possessed. If these people seek knowledge and research about spiritual subjects or the different ways of spirit communication, they might find some answers to the claims of being possessed etc.

Our five senses help us in everyday life so we can understand everything around us, and we are able to function within the environment in the form of touch, see, smell, taste and hear. When a paranormal activity happens, and any of our five senses cannot relate to these activities, we automatically create fear within our minds and panic because we lack the knowledge of spirit communication. If it was that simple for spirits to make us aware of their presence, we would not need mediums or psychics. Think about it? I fear some people in this world, let alone in the spirit world. I am sure your spirit family and friends would not let any harm come to you when they were on the earth, and I am sure they protect you in the spirit world. Have you ever told someone a story, and by the time the story gets back to you, everyone who listened and passed the story on to the next person adds their thoughts to the story? Of course, you have its human instinct to add their thoughts, just to make the story more exciting to listen to. I have been aware of spirits since childhood, and I have never met or seen a spirit that wants to harm me or anyone else; it's all in my mind. I have seen objects move without any physical help, and once I observed a pint glass rise to a height of ten metres and crash to the floor. This does not mean that spirit is trying to hurt me. If this happens to you, you will find that someone around you has a strong psychic gift, and this will create energy for the spirit to make contact. There's a wealth of spiritual knowledge that will provide you with answers to your questions, and any spiritual centre or reputable medium will help you and explain these types of paranormal experiences.

The difficulties and problems of communication with the spirit world are well known to every genuine medium, a person of whom devotes years of their lives to its development. Possession by an evil spirit assumes that such spirits are free to visit the earth and that they are not subject to the same difficulties of communication as those spirits of loftier intent. Both are incorrect and spiritualist teachings clearly state that misdirected spirits automatically gravitate to their appointed sphere of experience, there to learn from and reap the results of their actions. Spirit laws are constant and cannot be flouted, and the concept of possession by an evil spirit is the residue of medieval practises unfortunately preserved by ignorance. No individual subscribing to such beliefs can be a spiritualist and would be well-advised to study the laws and principles involved to understand that the fundamental message of spiritualism is one of beauty and love. There is a prevalent belief that evil entities roam the earth in search of opportunities to create havoc through unsuspecting people. A concept that has been "energised" by Christian Exorcism and superstitious beliefs, which belongs to the dark ages. In all my experience in my life and as a medium, I have never contacted such an entity, and it is preposterous to assume that the spiritual laws of the universe could be flouted in this manner. I have no fear of the DEAD but cannot say for the living!

In the process of growing up, a man attempted to rationalise his environment and, whilst still in his evolutionary infancy, formed certain concepts, the majority of which have long since been superseded in direct proportion to his capacity for ascertaining the truth. When I was a child, I say as a child, but now I am a man I have put aside childish things. However, some of these primitive ideas have survived as superstitions, particularly where the benefit of education is supposed or lacking. Evil was attributed to God, and the cure used by the priestly magicians was appeasement in the form of sacrifice. Deities proliferated, and Christian Devil is an amalgam of pre-existing concepts projected upon the pagan God pan complete with cloven hoofs. In our modern world, such superstition is an abomination to the Godhead, and mankind is still reaping the effects of this priestly error that has been perpetrated to enslave the minds and willpower of the gullible and weak. In recent years has the church attempted to use low key methods where its devilish doctrine is concerned, but 'what a tangled web we weave when first we practise to deceive'. Having invented the devil and his dominions, the church then had the effrontery to designate him the inventor of spiritualism. We can only assume that the church was trying to dispose of this untruly progeny, but the superstitions monstrosity can only be dissolved when its inventors are prepared to admit their grave error in retaining primitive doctrines in an attempt through fear to imprison the human family. At the end of the Middle Ages, the church started to lose its stranglehold upon European life with the collapse of medieval concepts, and the empty churches of today are proof that the liberating power of truth is deposing falsehood. It is natural for us to make mistakes in life, which is our teaching, and we learn from our mistakes. You don't need to be brainwashed into thinking that the devil is working within you when you make a mistake and that God will not forgive you. There is no such thing as the devil. It's a descriptive word of something you can relate to in order to put fear into you. The English Dictionary describes the word `Devil` with many meanings and is all about ``bad spirits``, where does this information come from. Over the years, I have encountered many spirits, and I have never met any bad spirits yet. I believe the devil does not exist; don't you think we have enough evil in our world at the moment, which is created by ourselves.

Spiritualism teaches that all life is in a state of progressive refinement and that the spiritual element in man is moving back along a pathway of experience towards its Divine Source. Inwardly man is the repository of infinite possibility, whilst outwardly he is the sum of all the hereditary forces which meet in him together with environmental and educational influences. Outside human consciousness, there is no problem of good and evil, a fact which reveals man's superiority of consciousness over the lower kingdom. He has already discovered that hormonal balance is achieved by the application of natural laws and will ultimately awaken to the fact that to achieve complete and integrated harmony, he must obey the laws of the spirit. It is when he transgresses the laws of his being that the pure forces of God are hindered, and effect is manifested as so-called evil.

Every infringement of spiritual law brings an adequate effect that guides him back to the pathway of progression. However, should the infringement be persistent and severe, in accordance with spiritual law, the individual gravitates after physical death to a spiritual sphere of existence to learn more and reap the results of such action. Variations of the hereditary, environmental, and educational processes interact with the individual willpower, and there are those whose heredity is a stronger influence than their environment and vice versa. Where the spiritual consciousness has begun to unfold, willpower is correspondingly strengthened, and the individual is able to resist the negative elements of misdirection whilst in another, poor environmental forces could inhibit the unfolding of spiritual consciousness. Praise and blame are, therefore, eliminated.

Man is slowly raising himself above the law of the jungle, as the benefits of his past physical, emotional, and mental development are now contributing to his spiritual enfoldment. This will result in an eventual recognition of the fact that lawbreakers are not responsible beings but are obeying forces that they have no power to combat, forces that reach back through all the subordinate kingdoms and are lost in the mists of pre-history. When society is sufficiently enlightened, such people will receive human treatment to awaken the higher spiritual nature, which, in the words of Andrew Jackson Davis, is buried beneath the psychic wreckage of prenatal influences.

Misdirection at the hereditary, environmental, and educational levels is the source of evil, the effects of which make man evil rather than an evil man. All universal creation, including man, receives and transmits the love of God to greater or lesser degrees according to the individual hormonal relationship with the Godhead. It is necessary, therefore, to pay special attention to our inner and outer relationship with each other as members of the human family and our position in the material and spiritual worlds, establishing thereby a union between the human and divine, which could raise the levels of human existence. The cure for evil can only be effected by removing the causes of misdirection!

People have reported that they have been scratched and bitten by poltergeist or objects thrown at them. Let us consider that man is always afraid of anything which he/she is unable to understand, and that fear can almost always be traced to a lack of knowledge. When all facts are known and understood, the fear element is replaced by one of natural curiosity and, consequently, personal growth. The tantrums of a naughty child have no mystery or fear for the experienced nanny, where knowledge and experience indicate the necessary action to take. It is generally felt amongst others in the spirit world that innocent activity is often misinterpreted in the physical world as a wilful entity when a simple attempt to attract attention may have been the only factor involved.

Natural laws are perfect, and every individual is subject to these laws, more so when thoughts of transgression, which may harm others, are involved. Such wilful spirits are contained entirely within their own `mansions` and are not free to roam our physical world. Consider also that specially trained spirits work amongst those of special need in this connection and to do their special work must descend to their special mansions or realm which involved.

Some people who are not aware of their psychic abilities release unconsciously psychic energy, which may become involved with what you call poltergeist activity, leading to further confusion. It is first to separate the different parts which may be involved. Already the mystery and fear begin to fade as the research for knowledge commences. When an item is raised above the frequency level of the physical world, it is invisible; it is invisible to you though fundamentally still part of the etheric sheath. In other words, the energy world from which the form world is created constantly recreates the world of forms. If you switch on an electric fan at a slow speed, you can see the fan blades moving around. If you increase the speed, you will not see the fan blades because they are moving faster than the earth's frequency. You will be able to see through the moving blades and see the back of the fan. However, you are aware that the fan blades are there, even though you cannot see them at this speed. Therefore, you can rationalise and understand, which in turn does not scare you. The point I am making is that there will be a simple explanation for any form of paranormal activity.

A Ghost or apparition has a very wide definition. When the physical body comes to an end, the energy (Spirit) leaves the physical body and enters another dimension that our five senses do not recognise. Energy cannot be destroyed; it only changes, I believe to a faster frequency. In my opinion, the word ghost is the same as spirit. Spirit in Latin means "breath", but also "soul", "courage". The soul is the immaterial part of a person. It is usually thought to consist of one's thoughts and personality and can be synonymous with the spirit mind.

Spirit Entities have often expressed the fact that they are attracted to the medium by light emanations of the aura. In this connection, the principle, `like attracts like, ` operates due to the law of attraction and repulsion. The numerous tales of `evil` spirits ensnaring unfortunate mediums is beyond comprehension in the light of auric science. According to spiritual enfoldment, there comes a refinement in the auric atmosphere together with a strengthening of spiritual power. The protective quality in the aura against unwanted influences is clearly established. The adage, birds of a feather flock together, is applicable, and if we desire to attract the higher intelligence from the world of spirit, it is vital that we pay attention to the quality of auric light being transmitted. Darkness always yields to light, and the beauty of the spiritually evolved aura cannot be presented by malicious entities. Besides attracting evolved spiritual beings, remember that the aura also protects from the lesser evolved spirits. When, however, the need is felt to assist these unfortunates in the way of spiritual service and love, the spiritual power of the developed aura is transmitted freely in the desire to help.

Chapter 14: My Spiritual Diary

In the early stages of development, it is advisable to keep notes of things that come to you both inside and outside of the circle. This will enable you to analyse the things you have done and spot any trends or repeat patterns, such as reoccurring images that may be symbolic in some way. It will also enable you to establish what disciplines work for you and which do not. Making notes enables you to keep track of the things that you have tried and what areas require further attention and work. If desired, a brief outline of the notes could also be kept in a diary as these record the chronology of your development.

At the time of writing these spiritual encounters, I had no idea why I had to write. I followed Spirits' instructions to record all these events; for what reason, I did not know until now. I believe these spiritual teachings are to be part of this book, to provide an insight into how and the many ways of spirit communication when working with us. These events may explain to those people who have encountered similar unexplained occurrences and help those people who want to develop their psychic gift. At the time, I did not understand what was happening to me. I looked for a logical explanation and ruled out all the things that could have happened naturally at the time of each event. After examining these events as they occurred, I realised there is an unseen force, or our sixth sense is being activated. I believe we all have had a psychic side since the day we were born.

If you read with concentration, you will start to understand more about spirit teaching methods, which have been provided for my spiritual knowledge and the development of spiritual mediumship. We all have psychic abilities, which in some people are powerful, and other people not so strong. These psychic senses can be developed to bring out the best in everyone, provided you believe 100% about psychic energies. Developing your psychic senses is a continuous lesson. It's a difficult long road to walk along, and not many people continue strengthening their psychic senses. The process of thoughts for mental mediumships or psychics has a relaxed mind and body. Clearing the mind can take time in our world, but in the world of energies, there is no time because everything is continuous. There is no rush to reach the end. It is not a sprint, but more like a marathon.

I realised that spirit was preparing my mind, taking away the bad thoughts that I had, helping me come to terms with my past and making me undo the mistakes that I had made during my earlier years. My life was about to change for the better. No, I am not religious, but I believe in God, the universal religion meaning 'Oneness, with all energy life forms.' I knew my life was about to change. I believe we all have a destiny, and what is meant to be will be. For me, life can only get better in a spiritual sense. As stated, I had a psychic gift from an early age but refused to acknowledge that I had a gift. Well, I say I refused, or maybe the spirit influence knew I was not ready to represent them. I will say, though, I feel happier, contented, and have learnt a valuable lesson to understand nature, animals, and fellow humans. I have a slight knowledge of the universe and understand the energies in our world. I have a different view on various subjects and try not to get involved with disputes or bad feelings towards anyone. I try to lead my life in the good possible way I can and respect all people on earth, and I am grateful for everything I receive.

During the early part of my development, I was instructed via my subconscious mind to start relaxing, which is a form of meditation. I did not know the reason, but I followed my instincts and sat quietly, relaxing and letting the day's thoughts enter my mind.

During that time, I was never tempted to use my gift openly or privately. Even though I was asked on many occasions, it did not interest me at the time. I had known spiritual knowledge. I would be asked by certain people if I had a spirit message for someone, politely, I said "no". I believe this was a test from spirit to see if I would let my ego take over and seek public acclaim. I was never tempted at any time during my psychic development to offer my spiritual services to the public or private readings. This was a crucial part of training, and the words kept on repeating in my mind, "The applause of the populace is soon spent, but the applause of the `unseen hosts` lasts forever". You need to be determined and not let anyone try to persuade you into demonstrating your psychic gift before you're ready, which could take several years or two years minimum. Spirit will provide you with limited information, and as you progress, they will increase their teachings. They don't want to overload your mind at the beginning. This is one of the reasons why you should not be tempted to provide any aspects of spiritual readings or spiritual healing.

The spirit teachers understand your levels of commitment, they know how far to take you, they will never put a burden on you, and they realise you have a physical life to lead on earth. As I mentioned, it is a long spiritual path to travel along. Suppose you believe and have the desire to help others and lead a life of helping others and respecting all God's creation. You are letting your inner spirit shine bright, and as they say, 'like attracts like'. Never be disheartened, be thankful you have been chosen to represent the unseen hosts.

25th Dec 05

I was lying on the bed looking at a large tree through the window. I heard a voice in a whisper. I could not make out what the voice said; however, I immediately felt a sense of deep relaxation, and a thought entered my mind, happy birthday David. Moments later, I felt strange sensations on my face near my mouth and nose. It was as if someone was stroking me like a mother would do to her child at bedtime. I immediately had a thought that this sensation was being created by my grandmother "Caroline", who had passed when I was 13 years of age. I had an overwhelming sense of emotions, sadness, and happiness. It felt like my spirited grandmother was in the same room, but no physical presence. My grandmother often looked after me when I was younger due to my mother's lack of care. It was a nice feeling, and eventually, I fell asleep.

9th Jan 06

I lay in bed, relaxed, and closed my eyes. Just before sleep, I observed coloured lights; even though my eyes were shut, they began to move from side to side like stars. A loud noise startled me, which seemed to come from the bathroom area. I got out of bed and checked the bathroom, I investigated the bathroom, and everything was as I had left it. I checked the house for intruders, but the house was

117

secure. Nobody in the physical had tried or entered the house at the time of the noise. I tried to search for an explanation as to why the noise had disturbed me. It dawned on me this was an act of spirit energies; well, I think so.

16th Jan 06

Laid down, relaxing, and eyes shut, after a short while, I observed faces In the dark, eyes still shut; they started to come towards me and then stopped. I could not identify these faces; they were strangers to me. I was placed in what seemed to be a bedroom, which was slowly rotating: the vision was blurred. I could make out old-style furniture, and I noticed several pictures on the wall. A single bed with covers on was positioned next to the wall in the corner of the room. The wallpaper was a striped pattern, running from the ceiling to the floor; these stripes were 1 inch, 3inch and 1 inch in thickness. The vision went on for a time. It was like watching TV or watching a theatre play. When I woke in the morning, the vision I had was still clear in my mind, and during the day, I researched family photographs. I did not understand why these people appeared in my thoughts when I was supposed to be asleep.

12th Feb 06

At 1815hrs, I attended a spiritual church for a clairvoyance evening. The female spirit medium opened the service with a prayer, followed by her philosophy. In her clairvoyance, the spirit medium asked if she could speak to me - I said "Yes." She informed me that a spirit Monk was standing to the right of my shoulder, wearing his habit and with no shoes on his feet. The Monk was just looking at me without saying a word. She then went on to say a female spirit was standing at the left side of me, and she seemed to be directing the Monk. The spirit medium asked if I was aware of the lady and the Monk when they were on earth, I replied `No`. The spirit medium went on to say the Monk had cleared the path in front of me for me to walk along, and he would be at my side, protecting and guiding me as I walked. The spirit medium again asked if I knew these spirits - I said `No`. She then said look into your family's history, and you will find they are part of my ancestors. The spirit medium stated they were both stood at my side protecting me.

I consulted my mother, Patricia Golden, about what the spirit medium had said to me. Mum stood there in shock and said, "You are not making this up, are you?" I said, "No, I am not." She told me it was her parents who had visited me when the spirit medium was speaking; Martin Golden and

Caroline Golden. Mum said her father was a religious monk and lived in a Monastery in Ireland before he left for England. The reason why he had left was a family matter. He moved to Whitworth Village, Lancashire, England and settled there, working in the local cotton mill and at that time, he met Caroline. Mum then said, when her father passed when she was a child. Her father asked to be buried in his 'habit' (monk attire), mum went on to say her parent was inseparable. I never knew my grandfather; he passed away before I was born. I knew my grandmother, who was a wonderful lady. I had many happy memories with her. This, for me, was conclusive evidence that we have spirit energies around us.

20th Feb 06

I was in the kitchen making a cup of tea, and around the kettle and the cups, I observed light coloured spots moving from side to side, which then appeared on the kitchen top. I had a sense of energy near myself. At this point, I moved my head from side to side, but the spots did not vanish. They remained there for approx. 2-3 seconds before they disappeared. I feel my spirit teachers were getting me accustomed to higher vibrations and making me aware of their presence.

23rd Feb 06

I was driving along the road near ASDA Superstore, Rochdale, where I approached a slight bend in the road. As I negotiated the bend, I was drawn to a sign on a wall reading, "Nosebag". This word stayed in my mind for a short while. Later, a friend and I were sitting at having dinner. In conversation, he mentioned a true story about a donkey ride he had in Blackpool a few days earlier. He went on to say the donkeys had a bag covering their mouths, and it seemed they were eating; he did not understand why they had a bag over their mouths. I told him it was a nosebag. I have never used the word 'Nosebag'. The only time I knew of the word was when spirit teachers placed this word in my thoughts. Spirit, I believe, was broadening my psychic senses.

8th Mar 2006

Two cups and a long sandwich plate were on the bedside cabinet near the bed. I placed the cups and the plate away from the bed to the far end of the cabinet, so I would not knock them over whilst I slept. During the night, I was disturbed by the sound of a clash; the cups had been moved. I thought I had knocked the cups and went back to sleep. The next morning, I looked at the position of the cups and realised that I couldn't have knocked them over. I felt the spirit teachers were showing that they could move physical items. I had no fear or any nervousness, I accepted that spirit was being to teach me to understand all types of communication, and they tested my personality.

12th Mar 06

I arrived at the spiritual centre on a Sunday morning; the weather was very bad with heavy snowfall, so the centre was not busy. Later in the day, I had this urge to go for a walk on the Pennine moors. (Blackstone Edge). I was walking underneath the motorway bridge behind Hollingworth Lake, Lancashire, England. As I went under the bridge, a thought entered my mind that someone in a vehicle would be waiting for me as I walked. Thirty minutes later, I arrived at an area named pylon alley and noticed a land rover type vehicle was parked with two people inside. A male and female were sat in the front of the vehicle. I acknowledged them and wished them well. I passed the vehicle, and it was started and drove off. It seemed the occupants were waiting for me to pass because of the narrow lane.

The thought I had earlier, I believe was spirit making me aware of my intuition, my psychic senses. Therefore, showing that thoughts are indeed powerful. I carried on walking with a smile, and it felt strange that the unseen host was looking out for me, wherever they were.

14th Mar 2006

Walking over the Blackstone Edge, Lancashire, England, on a windy, cold, wet day, I arrive at a roman road. I noticed a plaque with the words 'Aggin Medieval' at the foot of a pile of stones. The stones had been there for over 600 years, and I took the opportunity to rest and have a snack. I was looking down over the ground below, and suddenly tiny images of stars appeared, then within seconds, I heard a slight female voice. I stood up, expecting to see a group of people walking towards my position. After a few moments of surveying the area, I realised I was the only person on the hill. I continued to eat my lunch when again the tiny stars appeared, followed by a male's voice. Once again, I stood up, looked around and still I was alone. As soon as these occurrences happened, they left just as quick. Not thinking anyone of what I had experienced, I packed my rucksack and made my way down to the valley.

I knew what I had just experienced, and I was quite sure that I heard the two voices. It dawned on me it could have been the spirits of 'Aggins' Stones,' or it was spirit introducing me to the inner ear.

16th Mar 2006

I visited 'Aggin Medieval Stones' to see if I could hear anything usual again. It was a cold, windy, sleet day. As I sat there, I heard crowds of people walking and noises of heavily loaded wheels. There were shouting and odd screams as if someone had hurt themselves. I checked, and as expected, it was just myself on the moors. In my mind, there is no doubt I had been experiencing past events of people using the roman road to travel along. At this stage, I was aware that my psychic senses were becoming stronger. But I still had uncertainties.

20th Mar 2006

I was reading a book about spiritual, 'automatic writing,' this subject fascinated me. As I read, I noticed a colourful ray of light inches wide and about two feet long in a straight line from the position of the radiator. At the same time, a small, shaped ball of light appeared, I looked directly at the light, but it suddenly vanished. I continued to read with the feeling my friends in the unseen world was at my side.

21st Mar 2006

I was sitting in my friend's house, watching the Television, and I observed floating images in the lounge and a tickling sensation on my forehead. This lasted for approximately two seconds, and I had a sense of comfort. I became aware that my spirit teachers were touching me gently. It was as if someone was stroking my face in a kind, caring sensation.

Clairsentient, meaning; touching and sensing, maybe this was the start of sensing spirit, and the spirit touches felt like a strand of hair rolling down your face.

26th Mar 2006

I was sat down having a conversation with a lady called Wendy in the lounge of her house. I observed "briefly" little dots (stars). I continued with my conversation and dismissed the shaped dots. One hour later, I realised what had happened. The dots that I had seen were the same dots I experienced on the Moors a few days previously.

I went into the kitchen where my friends were. I did not experience anything further. I then walked into what used to be Lauren's bedroom before she passed over on 22nd March. I sat down in the chair next to some fashion twigs that were in a vase. I closed my eyes and still thought about what had happened. I heard a small bang, "like something falling onto the (wooden) floor. I looked at the twigs and noticed that one of the branches was moving up and down. The bouncing twig lasted for a brief period. I was the only person who sat in the room extension when this event happened.

Earlier that evening, Wendy and I had been to the local spiritual centre. The spiritual medium immediate spoke to Wendy. She was informed that a small female child was sitting at her side, at the same time Wendy experienced her hand being held by a small hand.

I believe Wendy's daughter Lauren who had passed away a few days earlier, came to reassure her that everything was okay.

28th Mar 2006

I went to the Dearnley Spiritual Church, and the Spirit Medium provided a message from a spirit male energy. The communicating spirit male apologies for his behaviour when he was on the earth. He then went on to say he was proud of me and gave the sign of thumbs. At the time, I could not understand who this spirit male energy was.

Sometimes we can have a blank mind at the time of spiritual reading. Often, though, most people manage to understand the spirit's message.

6th Apr 2006

On this cold, windy, rainy day, I took my dog Monty for a walk around Hollingworth Lake, Littleborough, Greater Manchester. I spoke to the spirits in a normal way. I suddenly thought of what the Spirit Medium had said to me previously regarding the spirit male energy. I could not think who this might be. Then the name just came into my mind. I shouted the name, 'Barry,' who was my father. He was never in my life as I grew older, so in time you forget.

This was my father's name, and it put a smile on my face. I never knew him much because of his ways, which was his choice. With my father not being there for my brothers and me, this was a sad time, and I felt lost. I forgive him because he had come to me and said some comforting words. Thank you.

My father provided proof that there is life after death. We all seek forgiveness when we have done something to hurt or upset someone. You still need forgiveness in the world of spirit. It's best to try and put right your wrongdoings whilst you are here on the earth.

11th Apr 2006

On this quiet evening, I was lying on my bed, reading a book named "On the Edge of the Etheric" I started to feel slight tickling sensations on my face arms. At the same time, I saw small crystallised colourful lights on my page of the book I was reading. A thought entered my mind about "Deja Vu." Sometimes in our life, we have come across situations or places and said to ourselves, "I have done this before". This is what we call "Deja Vu". This shows us that spirits are all around us. This is the reason why when a Medium gives a reading to a person, they mostly say dates, places, and situations. It seems to me that Spirits are trying to communicate to the individual at one point in their lives. Unfortunately, the individual does not know this until they say to themselves; I have been here before or done this before.

Later that same evening, I was about to fall asleep. A spirit face entered my mind, I found myself in the kitchen of a house. I walked into the next room, the lounge. As I passed the front door, there was what I describe a small rubbish bin rolling on the floor. I continued to enter the lounge and noticed a woman dressed in a green nurse's uniform, and laid beside her was a young female child. I turned around, and another female spirit energy was stood there looking at me.

There were no words exchanged, and I realised I was back in my bed. I came out of my sleep state and started to think about what had happened. I remember my spiritual travel experience, but I did not understand the meaning. At no time did I feel any threat or see any evil. I felt totally relaxed as I was in the spirit house.

12th Apr 2006

I started to read a book. "The Etheric Edge and Analyses of Psychic Communications." I felt touching sensations on my face and observed crystallised lights on the pages (one light). I sensed spirits were approving the book. Every time I pick up a book to read regarding spiritual subjects, my spirit teachers always touch my face, and thoughts enter my mind saying they approve of the book. I understood spirit wanted me to increase my knowledge, and they would be able to use the word content in my mind.

16th Apr 2006

I attended Spiritual Lyceum at Dearnley Church, Littleborough, Lancashire, England. During the service and having discussions on different subjects relating to spiritual topics, I felt a touching sensation on my left ear and felt there was a spirit presence standing behind me. We continued with the class, and I looked towards the large light blue wall in the building. Directly behind the conductor (Gladys). I observed a colourful shape in the form of a person. The colours were of gleaming purple/turquoise, which stayed for a short while, and gradually disappeared.

I knew at that moment that the spirit teacher approved of my spiritual lessons from fellow experienced spiritual people of all ages. Each of them brought valuable spiritual experiences, and I had the privilege to experience these lessons.

17th Apr 2006

I was lying on my bed reading my book (Analyses of Psychic Communications). As soon as I started to read, I felt sensations on my face ears for a brief period. Then the sensations started on my face and neck. Spirit teachers were approving - the book was okay to read.

20th Apr 2006

When I have a moment, I like to read about spiritual topics, which relaxes me. I felt slight touches on my forehead. I was the only person in the bedroom. I heard noises in the room. (Could be next door where the noises came from?). I stopped reading for a while, and the sensation went away. I continued to read again; the touching started again.

That evening I went to the open service at Spiritual Church, Dearnley. The Spirit Medium, Alan Webb, was providing a reading for a lady who was sitting on the bench in front of me. He suddenly stopped talking to the lady and said to me, "can I speak to you?" He asked me if I had known a young lady who had passed over to the spirit world when she was young (late teens, early twenties). I replied, "I cannot place this spirit". He then went on to say she was

130

standing near me and pointing down and saying, "he is my sweetheart". I said I could not place her. The Spirit medium then continued to speak to the lady in front of me. He had finished his reading with her, turned his attention back to me and said that the spirit female lady knew me. I remembered a friend named 'Rachel' had passed away recently at the time. I was absolutely thankful for the spirit medium, Mr Alan Webb.

At the time, I could not think of who this person was, not that I had forgotten her, but my mind went blank for some reason. Sometimes when receiving a message from the spirit, we forget about our past and cannot place the evidence. At some point, when the mind is relaxed, you will remember the communicating spirit.

21st Apr 2006

I was reading my book. As soon as I started to read, the touching sensations on my face and ears started again for a short while. I tried to communicate to the spirits and asked for their names, but I received no response, only their touches. I was very grateful for their presence. They were becoming part of me in a way.

23rd Apr 2006

I was lying on my bed reading a book named "Astral Projections"; I had a slight sensation of a touch on my face. Every time I picked up a book about a subject to do with spiritual subjects, the spirits came around me to confirm this was part of my teachings.

24th Apr 2006

I was at the meditation class at the Dearnley Spiritual Church, Littleborough, Lancashire, England. I experienced touching sensations around my face and ears. It seemed that someone was cleaning out my ears. Then I had a touching feeling at the left elbow up to my arm in a gentle fashion. I asked the spirits could they tell me if they were a male or female. I said if you're a male, could you touch me on my right cheek and if you're a female, could you touch me on my left cheek. Moments later, the spirit touched me on my right cheek. This tells me that the spirit was a male. I also had a very dry throat to the point I had to cough, and my eyes watered. My ears also continued to have a loud buzzing noise. I did get the feeling that the spirits were trying to develop my senses and making me aware of their presence.

25th Apr 2006

I lay on my bed reading my book. After a short time, I started receiving touching feelings on my face, feet, and arms. But they were very slight feelings.

2nd May 2006

I was laid on my bed meditating. I started to get touching sensations to the point that they tickled me in different places on my face. I then had a vision that was very brief. The vision was a spirited male and female who I cannot describe. The vision I had was mainly of a white plastic bag with beer cans inside. The owners of the bag were a young couple, and they were drinking the cans of beer in the spiritual centre. This spiritual vision was very clear but lacked descriptions of the couple. Maybe I should have asked for further information.

June Jackson of Dearnley Spiritual Centre confirmed that day she had problems with a man and woman who had been drinking in the building. She received a lot of verbal abuse from the couple, but in the end, they went on their way.

Spirits were making me aware of what was happening on the same day as they came to me. It is outstanding that I receive these powerful thoughts of energy with a message which can be transferred into our physical world.

133

4th May 2006

I started to read my new book titled "How to become a Psychic or Medium". As I lay on my bed, I had touching sensations on my head, face, eyes, and ears.

I stopped reading for about 10 minutes, the touching sensations stopped. I continued to read my book and the touching sensations started again. My room was quiet and warm, and there was no breeze in the room. As the touching feelings continued, I smelt tobacco a few times. The smell did not go away. It certainly was a communicating spirit, well I thought so. I tried and tried to think who I knew when they were on earth, and they smoked cigarettes. I could see, out of the corner of my eye, shadowy shapes of people moving around, which created a draught for me to smell the tobacco. When I stopped reading, the touching sensation stopped. The Spirits are getting stronger with me. I believe this spirit was someone who smoked when they were on the earth plane. I know one day it will come to me.

5th May 2006

I spoke to a friend on the mobile phone for about twenty minutes. When the conversation had ended, I went to the bathroom. I heard a lady's voice which was muffled. I immediately thought it was next door and that they must have come home from a night out, even though I did not hear them arrive home. At that point, my mother coughed in the next room. I knew it was not her voice I heard. I went back to bed and started to read my book as usual. The touching sensation started on my face. I stopped reading and put my book down, and the touching sensations stopped. The next morning my mother came into my bedroom and sat down on the bed. She told me that during the night, her mother, Caroline, had been standing in front of the dressing table in her bedroom, looking at her. She asked her mother why she was standing there, and then she told her spirited mother to go away. She then went back to sleep without a second thought.

I have asked in prayers for my spirited granddad and grandma to watch over their daughter, my mother. This confirms that the female's voice I heard was, in fact, my spirited grandma, Caroline Golden, trying to communicate with her daughter and me

7th May 2006

I attended Dearnley Spiritual Church, Littleborough, for the Divine Service with my friend. The spirit medium addressed me and said to me that the spirits told him that I had travelled the world. He said that there is a link to Pakistan and something about a 'jug'. In further conversation, he said there was a link between a brewery and me. At the time, I could not place this information. The 'brewery' is my new business name, "Brewery Management Services", and the link with Pakistan and the jug relate to my mother. Her landlord came around her house to repair the water system. He told my mother that he had a loose stomach and needed to go to the toilet. The landlord asked my mother for a jug of water so he could clean himself. The medium also mentioned that I had a link with Aldershot, Doncaster, and Scotland. I have been to these places whilst serving in the British Army.

8th May 2006

I went to the Closed Circle (development class). During the meditation, spirit energy came close to the left side of my body. I felt a slight force near the side of my face. At the same time, I shivered; it became cold within my immediate area. For some reason, I sensed it was the same spiritual energy that had been visiting me from the beginning of my development. I never felt threatened or afraid. As a matter of fact, I felt comfortable and relaxed.

At home, looking towards the bedroom window, I had a vision of a little girl's face that resembled Lauren, who had passed to spirit. She was visible for a few moments, and it appeared she was smiling. It gave me great comfort knowing that she was happy, and I knew she wanted me to let her mother know she was ok in her new surroundings.

14th May 2006

I was looking at a huge tree through the window and watched the birds singing. I shut my eyes as I lay there and immediately experienced a vision within my mind of a violet-coloured triangle that became bigger. Seconds later, images of spirit people appeared in what appeared to be a room. It seemed like a room in a house dating in the 1900s, which year was difficult to establish, then spirit energy came closer to the screen in my mind, I tried to concentrate on this spirit energy, but it went away just as quick then another spirit energy drew close, and the same happened again.

Later that day, I decided to relax and shut my eyes, the same violet screen appeared, and there were several spirit energies coming into my vision fast indeed. I could hear noise within my mind, but it seemed they were from another room. A spirit male energy with his back to me; he had light coloured hair at the sides of his head, he had a bald patch on his head. Then there were spirited children's energies. Their faces were blurred. I felt spirited female energy wearing what appeared to be a large earring in her left earlobe. She resembles my cousin Josie who had passed when I was thirteen years old.

Suddenly there were several spirit energies moving to the front of the screen in my mind, and they came faster and faster. I had the impression they were taking turns to look at me. I was moving my eyes, trying to capture each spirit's energy, but they were too fast for me to really grab a vision clearly, then a cream looking vase with flowers inside was shown to me. I sensed it was a versional gift from them to me, making me aware of their kindness.

Throughout this vision, the edges of the screen were the colour violet, and as quick as it came, it vanished, bringing me back to consciousness. The birds in the tree were still singing, which gave me the impression that my unexplained vision in my mind was for a few minutes or seconds. But during the mental vision, it seemed longer.

17th May 2006

I went to bed for the evening, relaxed. As soon as I closed my eyes, the Spirits touched my face, my ears, nose, mouth, and the top of my head. It felt that there were several spirits. I asked my Guardian to protect me. I started to see in my mind's eye little single bright white lights. These lights came at random from different parts of my mind's eye. I said good night to the spirits and went to sleep.

20th May 2006

I was on my bed that morning, reading a Spiritual Book about Automatic writing. I started to receive touches on my face, and at the mouth area, I put the book down and spoke

138

to the spirit's energy mentally. I closed my eyes, and in my mind's eye, I observed a beautiful colour of violet/blue and slight images. I could not make these images out; however, it was the spirit energies way of telling me that they were around me. I went for my breakfast with my mum in the front room. My mum had an Incense stick burning. The smoke started to follow me to my chair (it could have been a daft I created). I sat down, and the smoke started to drift upwards in a straight line. When I moved, the smoke followed me. Maybe my mind was working overtime, but I felt contented and relaxed throughout.

21st May 2006

I attended Dearnley, Spiritual Church, Divine Service. In church, I sat with two ladies named "June & Lynn". The female spirit medium told me that there is a lot of energy around me and that I have a musical background. She then said there is something to do with writing music and playing the organ. She then went on to say that I would be walking in the desert with sandals on and doing a lot of thinking. The spirit medium then said the spirits had built a pyramid around me with a lot of energy. She went on to say that a Native Indian chief was stood behind me, pushing me forward and that I was "Special," and the spirit energies have plans. She also mentioned young, spirited boy energy was dancing around me being happy. The spirit medium then said

that a spirit lady was with me and described her to be 5` 4"
tall, slim build stunning looking, long dark slightly curly
hair. She walked with grace, and she had a permanent smile.

A few days before I was in the spiritual centre café, I
made some enquiries about the electrical organ that was for
sale. I was informed that I could have it for free if I wanted
it. It confirmed the spirit medium's message.

In the afternoon, I went to the Cowboy Clobbers shop in
Heywood, Lancashire and bought two pairs of Cowboy
Boots; now I know the reason why I bought them before the
spirit medium came to me and told me those kind words.

I had touching sensations around my face. I knew the
spirit medium would speak to me, but I did not know what
she was going to say. Spirit will use all methods to convince
you they are teaching you, slowly and progressively, and
they were with me at the times when I was in the shop and
speaking about the electrical organ.

27th May 06

I was reading a spiritual book titled "Automatic
Writing". As I read, my vision went blurred. I observed
lights with tails moving around. A shadow of a person
moved from left to right near the bedroom window. The
answer came into my mind about a question I asked spirit

previously. Spirits will answer your questions when they are ready, and it's not always the answer you expect.

31st May 06

Mother and I attended Rochdale Infirmary Hospital to see mum's elder sister, Josie, who had been admitted. On the way to the hospital, mum said that my dad`s "auntie Mo" was in the same hospital ward as Josie. I spoke to "Mo" regarding my father (Barry) and asked if she could give me a photograph of him. At the same time, I had strong, touching sensations all over my face, and I told "Mo" that the spirits were with us. Mo just stared at me with her mouth wide open the look on her face was of shock. I realised some people don't accept life continues in another higher existence. Everyone has different views on this subject, and I learnt it was not my way to preach to others. If they ask, then I will say my views.

I was mediating later that day when I experienced spirit energies touching with force. It seemed there were several spirit energies. There was a slight breeze near my feet, and it seemed like I was being turned around, mentally, of course. I asked the close spirit energies which they were, I sense I did not know these spirits, and I quickly concluded they could have been mischief trying to anchor on to my energies.

4th June 06

On my bed in the afternoon and closed my eyes, shortly I observed the colour of Violet in my mind's eye. This started off as a small spot that grew larger. I had touching sensations all over my face. Spirit Teachers were just training my mind for development.

14th June 06

I was reading a book titled "The Phenomena of Spiritualism" at home. I started to receive touching sensations on my face and right ear. My left hand started to twitch slightly. Furthermore, I observed the movement of images in the room; these images were becoming stronger.

I felt the spirit energies were making me aware they were still with me, but having a break gave me time to adjust.

18th June 06

Mid-day, I was taking a rest and laid down to close my eyes. I lay there and could hear the heavy traffic outside my house. A mental vision was created of shaped circled spots, then a coloured wallpaper appeared. I was semi-conscious, and I could still hear the traffic outside.

During the day, I began to look at people in the street, and I could visualise their colourful aura and certainly their physical aura. I looked at my fingers because I had a tingling sensation in them. I placed the fingers of each hand in a vertical position and slowly brought them together. A few inches close, I could see a bridge of energy, like the sun's haze rising from the ground on a hot summer day.

25th June 06

Early that morning, I was lying down with my eyes shut. I started to see beautiful colours of patterns like clouds moving around and around for about 20-30minutes or so. I felt comfortable, contented and at peace within myself.

26th June 06

I attended Dearnley spiritual centre for the development circle. The leader of the circle asked if I would do the open prayer. I started with our father. Then my mind went blank, the group leader took over and said the prayer. At the same time, my spirit friends started to touch my face. They placed me in a spirit house and several spirit energies again. Spirit energy seemed to play hide and seek with me, then the chair I was sitting on started to vibrate from the rear. It lasted for a short while. I began to have a dry throat, and my eyes even closed became sensitive. I felt drained and began to breathe heavily. I felt I was being prepared for the communicating spirit energy to use my physical body for their purpose, for what I cannot say.

It was at this point the leader of the group asked the group to release from the spirit and slowly come back to our world. During this remarkable new spiritual experience, I had I felt comfortable and relaxed. I had no fear or upset. I believe the spirit energy was trusting me as I trusted them.

I did some research and learnt that spiritual energies could use ectoplasm to help them to be visual and for others. Your inner spirit at the time steps to one side of your physical body, and the communicating spirit step in while they communicate.

You must have total commitment and trust your inner self and the spirit energy; this type of mediumship is Physical mediumship. Physical mediumship was the main method of communication in the earlier days of spiritual phenomena.

31st June 06

My friend Lisa came around to my house for a chat. We were having a conversation in the front room. Lisa mentioned her spirited granddad and that she would like him to come to her one day. I explained he will when the time was right. After a few moments, Lisa suddenly became very scared, to the point she started to cry; she felt panicky. I asked her, "What is the matter?" She told me that she had felt a vibration that travelled through her physical body.

We continued to have a conversation, but Lisa was extremely upset. I realised she was in a panic state to the point she was going to run out of my house. I explained what had happened that our energies blended, which became strong, and your spirited granddad was able to come forward, and even though it seemed in a powerful way, it was not. It was the case that her spirited granddad was not used to coming forward often. She said she has never felt the spirit so strong, and I am the only person who has brought her spirited grandfather through. Lisa did not want to continue to speak about her granddad, so we changed the subject, and Lisa became calmer. She composed herself and felt relaxed.

This event had taught me a valuable lesson. I was inexperienced, and I should have taken control at the time of her spirit granddad coming forward. It is a lesson I will never forget, and I know now from this experience I must not allow spirits to draw close in my early development.

3rd July 06

Early in the morning, I was lying down with my eyes shut. My mind's eyes started to open. I experienced white coloured clouds and shadows. It was like an old picture film, an old cine camera film. This was very short; my mobile phone started to ring and brought me out of this experience.

When you meditate, always switch off your phones and try to make sure you are not disturbed.

16th July 06

I attended Dearnley Spiritual Church. The male spirit medium told me that the spirits have said that I am ready to work as a spirit medium and should not worry about spiritual Philosophy. He then went on to say that I should talk about my life experiences because they would help others. This was a nice message to receive from the spirit energies, but at this time, I do not think I am ready for working on behalf of the spirits. I do think they will let me know when the time is right to work on their behalf. This could be now, next week or years. It does not matter to me and the spirits because there is no time limit in the spirit world. I know they want me to become knowledgeable regarding spiritual subjects. Be patient; the spirit teacher will appear when the student is ready.

I am not disbelieving the spirit medium with him saying I should start working as a spirit medium. I needed confirmation from those in the unseen world to say when I was ready. It is an agreement I have with my spirit energy teachers.

20th July 06

Early this morning, I was awake but still in bed. I started to think about the problems that surrounded me regarding relationships. It was part of my life I did not understand. I started to read a book titled; "Silver Birch Anthology". As I began to read, I felt slight touching sensations on my face and my right ear. I put the book down and closed my eyes. Moments later, I had a vision of a fiery inferno, balls of raging fire. It was like someone had ignited a fire from within me. I came out of my meditation and analysed the spiritual event. I concluded I had a lot of anger within me to think about any sort of physical relationship. I needed to learn about myself, learn to like and love myself.

I sensed that the spirit energies were showing me how to clear my mind from all the bad experiences I had faced during my life. I realised who I was and not what people wanted me to be. It taught me how to be grateful for what I have, no not materialistic items. I mean inner love, kindness, and how to forgive. You cannot develop your true spiritual, psychic senses unless you learn to be true to yourself and to others.

21st July 06

I was driving my car from the `Gordon Riggs`, Garden Centre, Walsden, West Yorkshire. A thought entered my mind that I needed to go to Saddleworth Spiritual Church. Jane. I sat in church; two rows in front of us sat a lady. As I looked at her, I had touching sensations at the top of my head. I began to intake deep breaths, and at the same time, my lungs and heart felt heavy as I continued to look at the lady. The open circle was announced, and I addressed the lady. I told her about my heart and lungs and explained the feelings I had. She confirmed this and told me she had breathing problems. I told spirit had placed this condition on me, and she should go to the doctor for a check-up. She thanked me and said she was under treatment from her doctor. I thanked the lady and sat down.

Open Circle is for people who want to share their spiritual experiences without the pressure of working as a spiritual medium. It also enables you to receive confirmation and guidance when relying on spirit messages to strangers.

24th July 06

A female medium at Dearnley Spiritual Church - Divine Service told me that a Native American Chief was standing behind me, pushing me forward working with me. She then said spirits had put me in a pyramid for energy to build up

148

my awareness. I have had this message mentioned previously.

I had recently moved into a house which needed renovating. I decided when the house was finished. I would have a Shih Tzu dog. A couple of weeks went by, and still working on the house, a thought came into my mind regarding a Shih Tzu puppy. I made several enquiries on the internet and noticed an advert "Shih Tzu Puppy for sale." I contacted the Advertiser and asked if the dog was still for sale. This lady, named Pauline, described the dog to me and told me the price. She gave me her address, and I said to her I would be at her house within the hour. Before driving to Burnley, Lancashire, England, I stop at my local bank to get some cash.

I knocked on the front door, and this was answered by Pauline. She invited me inside and suggested that I go into the front room whilst she fetched the puppy. Pauline came into the room with the puppy, and I immediately said I would like him and handed her the money.

I had strong feelings this puppy was meant to be at my home. Pauline told me the dog's Pedigree name "RAINDANCE FUDGE MONTY". I sat there with my mouth wide open and then smiled. Pauline asked why I was smiling. I told her a long story about what the spiritual medium had said. I opened the car door, and Monty jumped straight into the car and sat on the front passenger seat. He was totally relaxed and sat there staring. During the journey back home, Monty never showed any distress that some dogs show when they leave their owners.

I feel the spirit medium was confirming the Native Americans because Monty's full title, "Raindance Fudge Monty." Happy days.

5th Aug 06

I was half asleep in bed when I heard a voice shouting my name: "David, David" the voice said. This made me alert. I checked the house, and all the doors and windows were locked. I became fully aware and thought someone was calling me. There was nobody in my house or outside. Only Monty and I were in the house. It was a usual occurrence that something would draw my attention.

10th Aug 06

I attended Dearnley Spiritual Church. This was a busy occasion because it was termed a Special Medium. The male spirit medium told me that I should trust and listen to what the spirits are telling me, and it will not be long before I publicly demonstrate my psychic gift to help others and reassure people that there is another dimension.

I understand and believe what the spirit medium had told me, but I had an agreement with my spirit energy teachers.

28th Aug 06

I attended Dearnley Spiritual Church for development close circle. We sang a hymn and said a prayer, then recited the seven principles. I started to receive touching sensations on my face, and I heard a faint sound of Bagpipes. A thought came into my mind about my uncle Phillip, who is in a residential home in Scotland. At the same time, I felt my left cheek being pushed upwards. This lasted for a few minutes. I then experienced a dark space and fast shadows moving around, lights and greyish images of what appeared as heads, but they were not clear. The touching feeling continued, and a thought came into my mind about Philosophy. I had to do this on a Thursday or Sunday at some point. During this meditation, I felt relaxed, heavy and at peace with myself. The leader then called time. I contacted my auntie Olga in Scotland to ask her how my uncle Phillip was. She told me his illness had become worse and treated her like a stranger. I feel our spirit family, Granddad Martin and Grandmother Caroline, making me aware of my Uncle Phillip's condition.

9th Sep 06

I attended Saddleworth Spiritual Church with my friend Lawrence Simms a spirit medium of thirty years. As we travelled by vehicle, we discussed spirits. In the church, the female spirit medium asked me if she could create a link with me. I said `yes`. She told me spirit said to her that I see Orbs, and I need to listen to them and always be aware when they draw close to me. She then went on to say. The spirits want me to get an old, styled watch with a winding arm. She said spirit wants me to pre-set the fingers to 8.20 and leave the winding arm pulled out. She said next time you look at the watch; the fingers will say 10.00 o'clock. This will be spirit moving the fingers of the watch. As the conversation came to an end, I thanked the spirit medium and said I would follow their instructions. The spirit medium ended the conversation and continued to provide messages for other people in the audience. As the spirit medium was working, I observed on the wall to the right of her a bright light and images. Moments later, a shadow of a spirit male appeared on the wall. I noticed he had a pointed nose, and he was wearing a hat. The spirit male kept looking at the medium as she demonstrated throughout the service. The female medium after the service told me that the spirit I had seen was her Guide named "Big Feller", and he always makes an appearance when she is working. We had a coffee in the church, and Lawrence asked me for a pen. I handed him my pen. Lawrence stirred at the pen as he grasped it, he suddenly let go, and he was perturbed. I asked him if he were ok. Lawrence said he felt the pen burning his hand, and he showed me the marks where the pen had been. He then told me that a soldier was marching around me with his rifle on guard. The two soldiers protecting me are my Army buddies, David Archer and Tony Francis. They both had taken their lives because of the upset of a relationship breakdown. This was a very eventful evening for me, to say the least. Always follow the instructions from spirit to confirm their evidence.

12th Sep 06

Lawrence and I went to Hebden Bridge Spiritual Church, and we sat at the back. The spirit male medium was providing messages to the congregation. The medium asked if he could speak to me, I said yes. He went on to say if at any time coldness came near me, don't be afraid because spirit monks are going to bring me over to the spirit world and return me. The spirit medium then explained a few other things to me. He ended the conversation and went to someone else. Again, Monks have been mentioned. My grandfather, Martin Golden, came to my mind straight away.

13th Sep 06

I arrived at Manchester Airport and waited in the departure lounge. I looked on the screens to see if I could see my flight information and noticed no details available. Time passed, and everyone was rushing around for their flights. I had touching sensations on my face from the spirits. A thought came into my mind about my flight; I was going to miss the plane. I asked a male employee, a staff member of the airport, regarding my flight. This male said I was in the wrong terminal. He directed me to the terminal where I should be for the flight to Spain. I arrived at the check-in point for the flight just on time and waited in the queue.

Spirits were showing me that they were with me and helping. I believe it was a lesson to follow your instincts. If I was not prompted by the unseen host, I would have missed my flight.

24th Sep 06

I arrived the address of Torrevieja, Spiritual Church, 1 Avenida, Torrevieja, Alicante, Spain. When I got there, the church was no longer at this address. A kind Lady at this now Restaurant provided me with a telephone number and said this is the number to the owner of the spiritualist church. I rang this number and left a message on the answering machine. A few days had passed when I received a call from a lady regarding my enquiries. This lady explained she had been in England for a few days, and she had just got my message. This lady told me she is the president of the Torrevieja Spiritualist Church. She then provided me with the correct address. Avenida, Jaca 31 San Luis 03184 Torrevieja. The next day I set off heading to the spiritualist church in Torrevieja. I had to travel 30km approximately and set off in plenty of time before the service started. However, I arrived in Torrevieja with my friend Sue and her children. We tried to locate the spiritualist church, to no avail. We could not speak Spanish and found it difficult to understand the directions given to us by the local Spanish people. An hour had passed, and time was becoming an issue because the church service was starting in thirty minutes. I sat in the car and relaxed my mind, and felt the presence of spirit. I felt they were placing directions to the spiritualist church into my mind, and in turn, I directed Sue, who was driving. As we approached a junction, the spirits would place thoughts into my mind, which told me the correct turning to take. We arrived at the spiritualist church, and I got out of the car. Sue and the children drove off, with the view to return after the service. As I entered the grounds of the church, I was aware of a spirit presence with me. The church door was ajar, and through the gap, I could see the church service had started. I was about to turn and walk away when an elderly lady beckoned me to enter. She said she was expecting me. This lady directed me to a seat. After the service had ended, the same elderly lady spoke to me and introduced herself as the president of the church. She then automatically showed me around the church grounds and the attached house. In further conversation, she said that I had been sent to her to take over the church. I said I was being guided to the church but did not know the answer. At this stage, Sue arrived with her children. I thanked the president and left the area. At this stage of my spiritual teaching, I did not understand why I had to locate this spiritual church and for what reason, I had to attend. Sometimes we do find it difficult to understand spirit messages. This is all about developing to learn how to understand.

5th Oct 06

I attended Dearnley Spiritual Church for the Open Circle. As I entered the building, a church member named Rose handed me a wristwatch in which you had to wind up manually. The type of watch I was instructed by the female medium at Saddleworth Spiritualist Church. This Silver watch was owned by an elderly lady who was a Spiritualist, and she passed to the spirit world many years ago. That evening just before retiring to bed, I set the watch to 8:20pm and left the winding arm out, as instructed from the spirit world in the message from the female spirit medium at Saddleworth Spiritualist Church. While sitting on my bed reading the Psychic News, Monty started to growl and looked towards the bedroom door. He then stopped. Seconds later, Monty started to growl again, looking in the same direction. Monty stopped growling, and we both fell asleep. In the morning, I was laid there, sending my thoughts to the spirit world. I got up and looked at the silver watch with its winding arm pulled out. It showed 1220am. I was amazed, and it was at this time Monty was restless and barking. It seemed he sensed we had a company of spirits.

6th Oct 06

Just before I got into bed, I again set the time to 820pm on the same wristwatch and left the winding arm positioned out. I placed the watch on the top of the cabinet next to the bed and went asleep. The next morning, I looked at the watch, and it showed the time of 1220am same as the previous day. I never once felt any threat from the spirits. It seemed another part of my psychic development. It was at this point I was starting to believe 100% that there are energy forces that cannot be explained in our language to suggest there is life in another dimension.

8th Oct 06

I attended Dearnley Spiritual Church for the Divine Service. The service started, and the spirit medium provided her philosophy. The Spirits in the church let me know they were around me by them touching my face and neck areas. I was sitting on a wooden bench at the back of the church and in front of my position was a purple carpet that went from my position towards the stage. I looked at the edge of the carpet and noticed a straight line like a torch beam appeared from the stage to where I was sitting, and then the light doubled and moved to the centre of the carpet. They were 1 ½ inches wide. One of the lights disappeared; I thought it was a reflection from the ceiling lights. At this point, the remaining light went diagonally across the carpet from the stage towards me then suddenly disappeared. Seconds later, a face-shaped appeared on the carpet, and it seemed to be looking in my direction. The face suddenly disappeared.

Three more spirit faces appeared on the carpet, all staring at me, then another face joined the group. I asked who they were but received no reply. They just stared at me without showing any expressions. The clairvoyance came to an end, and at the same time, those spirit face vanished.

It could be possible that the spirit energies were continuing to make me aware of their presence. It also gave me more confidence that there was an invisible source of energy in the form of the afterlife.

15th Oct 06

My mind had a vision of spiritual praying hands which are displayed in a spiritual centre. It resembles spiritual healing. I explained this to my Spiritualist Lyceum President named `Gladys`. She instantly provided me with a book about the understanding of praying hands, and she said they are healing hands. When I got home, I started to read the book that Gladys had given me. At the same time, the spirit made its presence. I thought it entered my mind. The spirit wanted me to do some philosophy about the experiences of my life, and someone close to me needed spiritual healing. I believe the healing energies were for my friend Wendy, who had lost her daughter Lauren only a few months ago.

Spiritual Lyceum is like a Sunday School, it is where you learn about spiritual topics, and you all have a fun time doing all kinds of dancing games. Basically, it is a social fun time.

16th Oct 06

I attended Dearnley Spiritual church for the psychic demonstration close circle. Our circle leader 'Linda,' invited me to open the development circle with a prayer using my own words. Prayer is a form of protection and spiritual thoughts for those who may need help in the earth world.

The name Tom entered my mind, and a vision of candles, followed by a touching sensation. The name John entered my mind. After the meditation, I asked if anyone in the development circle knew the two names and the candles. Nobody offered a response to my questions; I knew it meant something to someone who knew me.

When I saw my friend Jane Thom, I mentioned my experience in the development circle. She informed me that her father was called John Thom. However, she could not understand the candles.

It sometimes shows when a message comes through, they are like jigsaw pieces, and you have to fit them in the correct position, as in this case, John Thom.

22nd Oct 06

Jane Thom and I travelled to Saddleworth Spiritual Church by car for the 3 pm Divine Service. As we travelled, I said to Jane that she would receive a message today from the spirit world and that the spirits are always around us. In the spiritualist church, the spirit medium Doreen Hodkinson started to pass on messages to the audience. I observed spirit faces (blurred) on the white wall to her left side. One spirit face had a slim straight nose, pointed lips, with a moustache slanting down. His hair was short and neat and reminded me of Errol Flynn, the actor. I had the impression this spirit image was a professional type of gentleman, maybe a writer. The other mentioned spirit face was in the background, and the Errol Flynn look-alike was the point of focus. It could have been that the other spirit's face was helping with their energy to allow the main spirit to be seen clearly.

In the evening, Jane and I attended Dearnley Spiritual Church. I was asked to do the chairing for the service. The spirit medium "Connie Bridges" provided "Jane" a message from her father, Mr John Thom, and she mentioned the Candles. Jane then remembered what her father had meant.

My first message was accurate after all, and this boosted my confidence. Sometimes the recipient cannot place these messages, but never give up and don't make them fit. Don't forget I only spoke to Jane about the message I received in the development circle a few days earlier.

24th Oct 06

I was reading a book named "The Facts, Faiths and Frauds of Religious History" written by Emma Hardinge-Britten. At about 1020pm, Monty, my dog, started to growl, and he was looking towards the bedroom door. He sensed that a spirit was in the bedroom, and this was confirmed by me receiving sensations around my face and buzzing noises in my ears. When I stopped reading, the noises and sensations stopped, and Monty stopped growling.

161

I sent out my thoughts to the spirit world and thanked them for making us aware of their presence. I turned off the light and fell asleep.

26th Oct 06

In the morning, I took Monty for his usual walk around the lake. The weather conditions were bad with heavy rain and strong winds. I spoke to my spirit loved ones and friends to thank them for placing kind thoughts into my mind and sending out spiritual healing thoughts to all mankind. I also asked my spirit guides and helpers would they take me to the next stage in my spiritual teachings. This was wrong of me. Spirit decides when the time is right to go to the next level of development.

My friend, "Heather" was coming to Stockport to do a work course study. She was travelling from Carlisle and asked whether I would meet her at the Stockport Railway Station. She has never been to Stockport. I was waiting at the station for the arrival of my friend, and an elderly couple was walking past me, and I overheard the lady remark that her luggage was too heavy for her. Her arms were aching with the weight of the bags. Immediately I offered to carry her bag for her because the male was also carrying heavy luggage. I took her luggage to a waiting taxi, she thanked me for my help, and I went back to the station, feeling happy.

I greeted Heather as she got off her train, and within a few minutes, we located the building she had to be for her career course. Heather had a few minutes to spare, and it was at this point we went for a coffee at a café nearby. We were having a conversation about the various topics, and spirit drew close and provided a message for Heather.

I told Heather that the spirits had a single Red Rose for her. Heather smiled and said that "Gary", her boyfriend, had sent a single Red Rose to her works two days ago; this embarrassed her. I continued to provide evidence for Heather, and she was very happy and understood the spirit messages, and now she can relax a lot more.

Later in the afternoon, Lawrence Simms and I set off to Blackburn Spiritual Church. However, due to the heavy traffic, we were unable to continue with our journey. We both decided to go to Dearnley Spiritual Church for the open circle. The open circle was announced; I provided a message from spirit for a Scottish Lady who was sitting in the congregation. She confirmed this message and thanked me. Just as I was about to sit down, the spirits sent another message for a female, where I told her to stop the crying now and enjoy life. She confirmed this and told me that she was crying that morning regarding her late husband. These were my first two messages in public. I had no nerves, just a sense of calmness all around me. Spirit will always look after you,

163

and they will not let you down. You must trust them 100%. I was not meant to go to Blackburn Spiritualist Church for a reason; Spirit wanted me to go to Dearnley Spiritualist Church to provide them messages because those two ladies needed help.

Always follow your instincts, it was the main reason why we travelled to Dearnley Spiritual Centre. An open circle is where like-minded spiritual people can provide spirit messages if they wish to do so.

28th Oct 2006

I was having a drink of tea with mum Patricia Golden, and mum mentioned her father and mother, who are in spirit. I informed mum that her father often comes around me and that he watches over her. Mother said I have a similar way to her father, and she believes he does come around me. I had a strong impression that mother has natural psychic senses, and she hears and sees visions of spirit. Mum has never used her gift to pass on the message to others. She leads her life as best as she can.

Lawrence and I attended the Saddleworth Spiritual Church that evening for the Open Circle Service. As we were waiting in the church, the Chairman informed Lawrence and me that the spirit Medium had not arrived and asked if we would do the service. Lawrence said yes but wanted me to do the opening prayer and the Philosophy. Whilst we were waiting on stage, a lady walked into the church and sat down instantly. There was a link between us. The Spirits started to touch my face to let me know they had a message for her. The service started with me doing the opening prayer and the Philosophy. Once I had finished, Lawrence demonstrated his spirit mediumship.

The Chairman announced that it was now the Open circle; however, nobody wanted to pass on any messages. As the service was concluding, I asked the Chairman if I could quickly pass a message, he said yes. I spoke to the lady with who I had a link and said some comforting words to her from Spirit loved ones. I provided evidence for her of a spirit family member who was with her and confirmed that she was in a worrying situation. After the service had ended, I walked past the lady to who I had spoken.

This lady quickly told me she was very pleased to receive the spiritual message and thanked me and my spirit guides for their help. It was what she had needed because she had found out her mother was being treated for cancer.

Sometimes the spirit impression is very strong to the point you will deliver the message. Well, I decided to venture down this spiritual path, so I have to agree.

1st Nov 2006

I was reading a spiritual book named "Automatic Writing. I heard a loud noise from the area of my desk in the front bedroom. I knew it was a visitor from the spirit world of energies. My thought was directed to them. I turned, switched off the lights, and stared at the wall near the window. I could make out a spirit person with sunken eyes, a slender nose, and a rounded head. I asked who he was, but I received no indication as to who he was and why he was there looking at me.

I had no fear of this visiting spirit, nor was I afraid. I sent my thoughts of love to him, and as I did, he slowly disappeared. You must remove all thoughts of evil entities and believe there are no evil spirits. Ghost is just another descriptive word that is used to scare people.

7th Nov 2006

I walked around Hollingworth Lake, Littleborough, with my dog Monty and started to have a conversation with my spiritual family and friends. I did something that the spirits disagreed with. I sent out my thoughts of apology and asked for their forgiveness, which they did by sending kind thoughts. I walked past the local Café for breakfast and sat near the window overlooking the lake.

Four people were sitting at the table next to me, and I overheard them talking about Muslims. The conversation was unpleasant, to say the least. They are comparing the Muslim faith with the faith of Christianity. They went on to say that Christmas cards are changing because of the Muslim beliefs, they suggested we all should stand up, and Christians should stick together. In further conversation, the group said the Muslims were trying to take over Great Britain.

I believe it is one of the reasons why world wars are started by different religious views. All religions mention spirit in their holy book, and in my opinion, no one is better than the other. When we die, it is the same process for everyone. We all go back to the earth and to the universe. It's the leaders of the countries that create these wars, having political disagreements which result in innocent men and women fighting, killing each other, and for what. You would have thought humanity would have learnt the lessons. Wars and destruction do not solve anything. It only brings pain suffering to many families.

I believe today's lesson is another way of developing my spiritual senses understanding what life means. Let's understand one another instead of fighting. I believe that the spirits guided me to this café and for me to listen to those people. Spiritual means leading your life in the best possible way, learning to love and forgive. Respect all lifeforms.

167

Being spiritual is not part of any religion. It is part of the creation of the universe. It's part of all creatures, great and small. If you cannot forgive, how can you truly love? Leading a good life on earth is the true powerful link to the spirit world of energies.

8th Nov 2006

I attended Whitefield Spiritual Church for the open circle. When the open circle was announced, "Doreen", my developing class teacher asked if I had any messages to pass on. I walked to the front of the church, and as I did, spirits were touching my body, mainly around my face. I was directed to a female in the congregation and asked for permission to speak to her. She said yes. I described a spirit family member and a spirit friend named "Sandra", who had passed into the spirit world of energies. She confirmed her spirit family member, and she knew the name "Sandra", who was her best friend. After the service, this lady approached me and said that the evidence she received meant a lot to her. In further conversation, she became upset, then explained when Sandra died, she did not have the chance to say goodbye to her, and she carried this guilt for some time until now.

When spirit messages come through, they can be personal to the recipient. You may not understand what your message is when being passed on. You must always mention the first thought that comes to your mind and mention it. It will mean something to the recipient.

9th Nov 2006

Lawrence and I attended Dewsbury Spiritual Church for the Open Circle. Lawrence demonstrated and provided a message to a male in the congregation. As the evening progressed, I started to receive spirit touching sensation on my face. This made me stand up and provide philosophy, and I selected a couple of members who had never been to a spiritualist church before and explained about spiritual topics. I then was directed to another member of the audience and presented them with evidence from their spirit family members, along with a message.

After the service, a female committee member asked if I did "services" and would I do a service for them. I said not at the moment and explained why I could not take a service at their church. I mentioned to her I was in developing class at Whitefield Spiritual Church, and I did not have permission or directed by my spirit helpers to take any service at this stage in my development. I suggested that they ask my friend Lawrence to do the service. Lawrence asked if I would do the Prayer and the Philosophy, I accepted.

I had given messages in open circles because it was less daunting, and I felt relaxed. You only provide one or two messages as a rule. It was introductory for me to gain knowledge and have the feel of standing in front of an audience with no script and relying on the spirit communicators. Developing your spiritual senses takes time to prepare. It is something you cannot rush. It is a long term commitment.

10th Nov 2006

I was walking around Hollingworth Lake, Littleborough, with Monty. I asked my spirit family, guides, and helpers should have taken the service at Dewsbury Spiritualist Church. Moments later, as I walked around the lake, a thought entered my mind and confirmed I was not ready for demonstrating mediumship to the public on a big stage. I must remain patient and continue with my spiritual development.

There will be many opportunities to tempt you to start demonstrating your spiritual mediumship before your spirit teachers inform you are ready to serve. Lots have risen quickly, but to have fallen just as quick. You cannot deceive the spiritual teachers or guides; they know before you do what your intention is. If you do decide to demonstrate your spiritual gift, you will find your spirit teachers will stop working with you until you stop demonstrating. Spiritual is being truthful, and it is the only way to represent the spirit world of energies.

15th Nov 06

I attended Whitefield Spiritualist Church for the open circle. The open circle was announced, and I stood up and addressed the congregation. I mentioned the "Matrix Film", five members of the congregation put their hands up to accept this message. I observed a light pointing to a couple who were sitting at the back of the church. The couple told me they only had watched the Matrix Film the day before, and I explained to them what this meant. We then spoke about the telephone and the constant ringing, but no one was on the other end of the telephone. There were mentions of a dog whistle being blown, which the couple accepted and explained why.

After the service, the couple told me that her daughter's mobile phone had rung the house telephone. However, her daughter was standing next to her, and the mobile phone was on the table. They also confirmed they often heard a dog whistle, and they did not understand some of the strange things that happened in their house. Spirit will use an electrical item to draw your attention. After all, we have an aura around in the form of an electromagnetic field, just like the earth and all living energies.

16th Nov 06

Lawrence and I travelled to Huddersfield Spiritual Church by car. As we were travelling, Lawrence said to me that our spirit helpers had just told him that I should slow down and be patient regarding my spiritual development. The spirit medium at the church confirmed to me what Lawrence had said. I should develop longer before I do stage work. She also said my spiritual teacher is working stronger with me. She then provided me with proof of this.

Again, spirit making sure I am not tempted to demonstrate in public. Mind you, I was nearly tempted, but I never took the opportunity. I know how committed I am and trust my inner spirit.

21st Nov 2006

In Doreen's development class, you must learn how to demonstrate off the platform in a smooth, professional manner, and this is a practice in our development. I found this difficult at the time and felt my spirit teachers was not with me. All sorts of situations entered my mind. Example: what am I going to say? What will the public think about me? I started with stops and starts; I felt I was not making any sense. Doreen explained spirits are making me work by

172

stretching my mind, and they were testing me. This was a valuable lesson for me to learn. Always be honest and do not make stories up or fabricate evidence and claim it came from spirits. During your development, there will be times when spirits are not working with you; these are one of their tests to see if you will be honest and tell the truth. I cannot stress enough the importance of honesty.

22nd Nov 2006

Jane Thom, Lawrence Simms, and I attended Whitefield Spiritual Church for the Open Circle. Jane and I received a joint message from the female medium, which was nice about our friendship. When the open circle was announced, "Peter Clarke," who was chairing, asked if I had a message. I got up and addressed the congregation. I did not know who I had a message for; however, when I mentioned the message to the congregation, no one could take this message. Seconds later, the female spirit medium took my message from spirit. I feel that the female medium was helping me and am not too sure if the message was for her. Sometimes people cannot remember things from the past in an instant, and some people are too embarrassed to speak in front of people. I knew the message was from spirit. I also learnt that when people say the word `no`, they are saying `no` to the spirit's message and not to you personally. Jane and I were in my house in the kitchen area. In conversation, she asked me what her spirit message meant. I explained I could not elaborate on what the female spirit medium had told her. Jane needed to hear the message from the spirit, so I sent my thoughts to the spirit host, asking for help for Jane. I was waking up by seeing bright coloured shapes in my mind's eye. They were squares, triangles, rectangles, circles. These shapes came close to my face; I was then placed in a room.

The next morning, I tried to remember the spiritual place where I was but could not remember. I could remember the colours of the shapes. I believe that the spirits came very close. What the coloured shapes meant, I do not know. In time I will understand.

Always write down your dreams soon as you wake up; otherwise, you will forget your dream. I always have a pencil and paper at my bedside, which I can write down my dream as it is still in my mind.

25th Nov 2006

Lawrence Simms and I went to Leigh Spiritual Church and met other members of our development class. Doreen informed us we were all doing the clairvoyance service, and in turn, we had to provide a message. Each message would last for ten minutes, so everyone could have the experience of demonstrating to the public. I provided a message to a male and provided evidence regarding a tree and gardening.

The male confirmed he understood the message. He mentioned he had been in his garden working the day before. I then went on to say things about his lifestyle; the male confirmed the message. I left him with the love of spirit.

I then had a link with another male and told him a spirit male who had taken his own life draws close to him. The male confirmed that he knew the person. I then pass the special message to this male. He sat there looking at me with gratitude. I left him with the Love of Spirit.

I was about to do the closing prayer when I saw a colourful light from the church platform pointing to a lady in the congregation. I knew this was a spirit indication; they wanted to speak to her. I could not pass a message on to her because the chairperson had called time, and it's important to follow the chairing person's instructions. This was my first time on a platform working as a spirit fledging medium. The feeling I had felt was unexplainable. I was excited and knew this was the beginning of my destiny as a spirit medium. I trust and know that the communion of spirit helpers is working with me, and it is an honour to represent them.

28th Nov 2006

I arrived at Whitefield Spiritualist Church for our development class. It was my turn to work off the stage. I addressed the group and asked if I could speak to Sarah, who is also developing her psychic gift. Sarah said yes then I relayed the message from spirit for her. Sarah confirmed what I had said was correct and thanked me for the message. In Doreen's development class, her students must work off stage. It is to teach the student the familiarise of working in front of people, by using members of the development class.

Before I approached the stage, I observed faint faces on the blue wall and a green colour near the Christmas hamper. I mentioned this to Doreen, and she said that it spirits pioneers of the church, and they were helping us to develop. The energy in the class is always at its strongest.

29th Nov 2006

I attended Whitefield Spiritual Church for the open circle. The spirit medium (David Traynor) provided evidential messages to members of the congregation. When the open circle was announced, "Peter Clarke," who was chairing, asked if I had a message to give. I addressed the congregation and spoke to a male about the message from spirit in relation to his life and described the communicating spirit. The male confirmed what I had to say.

After the service, David Traynor asked if he could speak to me. He told me that the message I had provided for males he could also relate to. I thanked him for his kind words. The lesson I learnt, when you provide a message to someone, it also could mean something to someone else. Now, if I give the message, I know that it could be for more than one person.

30th Nov 2006

I was on laid my bed when my spiritual mind opened. I observed a male spirit of 6` 3" tall, Shoulder length dark hair, longish beard, and wearing camouflage clothes, with fur boots and his trousers tucked inside his boots. He was leaning on what appeared to be a 'log cabin door.' I looked at him and was about to ask what's his name. Before I could speak, he dashed off into the forest out of sight. He moved very quickly for such a big man. I know there is a reason why I have seen this chap, and one day I will have my answer. My development teacher informed me that I was not ready to be introduced to the spirit male; that's why he ran off.

3rd Dec 2006

I was sat on my sofa watching television and eating my dinner. I looked up towards my front window, which had vertical blinds. I saw a large shadow of a person. The shadow walked across the window. I got up, walked to the window, looked out and noticed that there were no streetlights on and no one walking near my house. It seemed I had been visited by a spirit male who was looking over me as I sat alone in the lounge of my house.

6th Dec 2006

Lawrence Simms, Monty (dog) and I went to Whitefield Spiritual Church for the open circle service. Monty went around the church, getting to know his new surroundings, suddenly his movement increased, and at the same time, he was sniffing the air. When the service began, I put the lead around Monty's neck, and as the service progressed, Monty started to growl towards the back of a lady named; "Janet". She was sitting in front of me. Monty then started to scratch the back of her chair, growling. At the same time, his attention turned towards the ceiling, and no one seemed to mind. The spirit medium was called to time, and the open circle was announced. Monty and I addressed the congregation and apologised for Monty's behaviour. I explained that Monty is aware of spirits, and he growls when spirits are around, especially at my home. I offered the message to the audience immediately. Two ladies acknowledged, and they both could understand what I had said. I asked mentally for further evidence from spirit. One of the Ladies could not take the evidence, so I thanked her for her link.

I worked with the remaining lady and continued to provide evidence for her. It was established the message was from a spirit loved one. I then went on to say about her life situation, regarding she had just had an argument with a friend two days ago. I described her grandmother to her, and she confirmed this. I explained that her grandmother was very happy, and she was making me smile. The female started to laugh. I told her grandmother was very proud of her, and she put her thumbs up regarding the argument. The female agreed on this. I thanked her for her link.

9th Dec 06

Monty and I went for a walk on Blackstone Edge, Roman Road, Littleborough Lancashire, England. When we arrived at the top of the Roman Road, I had a conversation with the spirit. I was making my way back down the Roman Road when I heard faint voices that sounded like a group of people. I looked around, and there were walkers about one mile away and travelling in the opposite direction. I believe the voices that I had heard were from the spirit world because there were no persons near my location. It was just shapes and shadows in my vision, transparent coloured dots just above my head.

I continued to walk down the road, and a thought came into my mind about the Queen, Princess Diana and the driver

179

of the Princess's car that had crashed. I asked mentally for further information, and I received touching sensations on my face. There was no further evidence given at this stage. However, I asked if that was the Spirit of Princess Diana and said I needed more evidence to establish if that was her. I then received a smile upon my face as if a spirit was laughing. I then received a thought when I was living at Flat 3 Oxford Place, Oxford Road, Manchester. The day Princess Diana had died, early that morning, I was woken up by someone pushing me in the back; I was in the flat alone. I walked into the lounge and switched on the T.V. The NEWS was about Princess Diana and Dodi they had been in a car accident in Paris, France, which was fatal. I am inexperienced at this stage to understand what was being said to me. However, I do know that all information from the communicating spirits needs to be checked and confirmed. There are some spirits who will relay false information and impersonate other people, especially public figures.

15th Dec 2006

Lawrence and I attended Barnsley Spiritual Church for the open circle service. In turn, each potential fledging medium addressed the audience and provided messages to selected recipients. I addressed the open circle and provided philosophy about; "do not give up" I mentioned three names the Queen, Princess Diana, and Dodi and asked if anyone

180

could take these names or had memorabilia of the Royal Family. Three members of the congregation said yes. I mentally asked for further evidence and mentioned western movies. One of the female members took this evidence, and I asked if I could work with her, she said yes. I told her that the Philosophy that I had said was meant for her not to give up. She knew what I was relating to and explained. I said that the cowboys and Indians are in relation to her Native American guide, and she has the ability for providing spiritual healing. She confirmed this and told me she was a healer but had stopped due to her husband becoming seriously ill. I thanked the lady for the link.

I had the chance again to address the open circle and started with a philosophy titled "Don't get angry". I mentioned that someone in the room had a serious discussion with a neighbour in the last few days. A male acknowledged and confirmed that he had a serious discussion with a neighbour. He went on to say he has been put through torment for the last eleven months. I explained to him that he needs to forgive and forget and move on. This male again became angry, and it was clear that he did not want to forgive. The name "Norman Wisdom" came into my mind, and I asked the male if he knew him. He replied yes. I explained this was for humour, the male then laughed. I told him that he had been given a jester hat from the spirit communicator. If the male did not relate to Norman Wisdom, then I would break the link and speak to the other members of the open circle. Later, An elderly female approached me and said that she was a friend of Norman Wisdom.

The lesson I learned was that sometimes spirits provide evidence for someone else, and they wanted me to break contact with the male and speak to this female. This shows I have a lot to learn when working with spirit. It is nice to receive a compliment for the evidence you provide, this gives you encouragement to continue, and it makes you aware that you are on the right pathway of spiritual growth. I always thank the spirit after for their hard work and always mention we are a team and there is no "I" in the team.

13th Dec 06

Lawrence and I attended Whitefield Spiritual Church for the open circle. The male spirit medium provided a link with me and said that I have to trust the spirits and that my guides have changed over. He also confirmed that I am spiritually aware, and no matter how small the message, I pass it on to the recipient because it will mean something to them. The Open circle was announced. Peter Clarke, who was chairing the service, asked if I had a message. I got up and addressed the audience, and asked if I could speak to the Asian couple.

They said yes. I informed them that I had a spirit male named Raj and described him. They both confirmed who Raj was. I then went on to say that Raj said welcome and repeated this. I informed the couple that's all he was saying was welcome. I thanked them for their link.

I then spoke to the medium `Mike Sheldrake, ` and said a spirit male named "Robert," The medium said he could take this. I then went on to say that the medium is still grieving regarding a passing over and that he puts on a front, but he is lonely and not happy underneath. I told him that Robert (Spirit Loved One) wants him to remember him when he was in his prime of health and not before he passed over to the Spirit World and that he is happy now and free. The name Cilla Black, Ken Dodd and Stan Boardman are named for upliftment. I thanked the medium for his link and left him with the love of spirit. After the service, the Asian Couple approached and thanked me for their message, and they were inspired to return. The medium thanked me for his message and confirmed the communicating spirit.

15th Dec 06

My friend, Darren Smith, and I decided to have a social evening in Manchester City Centre. We went into a Public House named "The Peveril of the Peak" we entered into the lounge bar area, which was very crowded. Darren suggested we go into the games room because it was not crowded, and we would get served quickly. As the young barmaid served us, I picked up a beer mat off the bar and turned it over. I began to read the advert on the mat and turned it over. There was a message written in a blue biro pen. It read, "Dave, you will meet a girl named Michelle tonight, good luck". I showed Darren the message, and we busted out laughing and thought no more of it. During the evening, we had visited several public houses and chatted with several people. At about 1 am, we decide to go to the Ritz Night Club. The Ritz Night Club used to be one of our haunts, and we thought it would be nice to visit. I approached the bar and bought some drinks. At the same time, Darren went to the toilet. When he came back, I said to him, let go and stand near the dance floor. A lady was dancing in front of us and was extremely hyper. She stopped dancing and stood near us. We exchanged conversations. I asked the lady what's her name. She replied, "Michelle," Darren's mouth went wide open and said, "My head is done in now", and he could not believe what had happened. In conversation, Michelle said that she is spiritual, and mediums visit her house on a regular basis. At this stage, Darren just stood there in total amazement. I explained to the lady what had happened early that evening. She understood. Michelle told us she goes to Altrincham Spiritual Church occasionally and asked if I have demonstrated there. I said no, but I know in the not too far

184

distant future I will be. In further conversation, Michelle asked me for my phone number so she could contact me for future reference. I said we would meet one day again at Altrincham Spiritual Church, she agreed, and we went our separate ways. Darren knows I am a spirit medium now; however, I never mentioned it to him in the past about my abilities. He now asks me questions regarding the spirits. But Darren is one of those people who need absolute proof from Spirits for him to believe. Darren asked me why this situation had happened tonight. I told him the reason why this has happened was to show him that there is a spirit world of energies, and we don't die. I also said that he is a kind-hearted man who has respect for everyone, and he is always offering help to those who need it. Spirit wanted him to know I am a spirit medium, and this is my new life.

20th Dec 06

I attended Whitefield Spiritual Church for the fledging mediums candle service, which I was part of. Each of us had ten minutes to demonstrate under the guidance of our development teacher Doreen. I was inspired to talk about Christmas, which lasted for twenty minutes. I was drawn to a female in the audience and asked her if I could create a link. She replied yes. I went on to say that a spirit male described him to her for her recognition. She confirmed this spirit male. This spirit male then went on to mention her personality and that it was her time to be happy. I then explained a small spirit dog came around her. She looked at me intensely and confirmed the spirit dog. I went on to say that she was about to visit the dentist for a check-up and to have a couple of fillings. This lady again confirmed this. I said thank you for her link and left her with the love of spirit.

23rd Dec 06

I went for a walk with Monty on the Pennine Moors in Littleborough, Lancashire. I selected an area near some stones and made myself comfortable and meditated. I started to feel a touching sensation upon my face near the left temple of my forehead. This was a stroking feeling which ran down the left side of my jawline. Moments later, I felt both cheeks on my face being pushed in the upward direction creating a smile. This lasted for one minute. At the same time, I had the sense of a spirit presence standing next to me. This was indicated by a slight pressure of energy to the left side of my body. I asked for the spirit to provide his/her name. I did not receive any answer to my question other than a sense of welcome. When I came out of meditation, I felt humbled and extremely happy and contented. Where I sat to meditate, I noticed ruins of an old building and maybe the spirit was the owner of the building or someone who lived there when they were in the physical world. It gives you an example that spirits can draw close to you in any environment, and you can meditate at anytime and anywhere.

25th Dec 06

Today is my birthday, and I decided to visit Dearnley Spiritual Church, Littleborough, to spend time with the spirits of the church. I sat in silence on a chair located on the platform. I was the only person in the church, and all the doors were locked from the inside. After a few minutes, spirits started to touch my face and continuously knocked on the wall to the left side of the stage. I got up to investigate and approached the area of the knocking. The knocking stopped. I went back to my chair and sat down; the knocking started again, which lasted for five minutes whilst I sat in silence. I did ask who was knocking; I received no answer to my question. I then felt a presence around me which indicated a spirit male of 5` 11" tall, medium build, long nose, grey swept-back hair and long grey sideburns. He was wearing what appeared to be working clothes. They looked like black trousers, black waistcoats, a shirt with no collier, hard-wearing shoes and a flat cap. I did not receive any information from this spirit male. This lasted for a brief time only. The energy slowly disappeared. On the rear wall of the church, shadows of shapes appeared. They were black in colour and in the shape of triangle, square, circle, and rectangle. These shapes would move around the wall at speed dashing from one position to another. I did not understand these images. One hour later, I said thank you to my spirit friends and left the church and handed the keys back to the caretaker, who was in his house next door. I later found out this building used to be a workhouse back in the early 1900s, and the spirit male, I feel he had a terrible accident in the main hall of the church near the platform.

26th Dec 06

Jane had invited me to have dinner at her house with her family. Jane's daughter Becky aged 16 was sat next to me on the couch in the front room. As I spoke to her, I observed a red mist around her. The colour red at this time indicated a special person, and she will be spiritually gifted. I never mentioned this to Becky because I was told she is frightened of unseen hosts. I would never impose on anyone, even though Becky knows I am a spirit medium. Later that day, Becky showed me photographs of when she was younger. I observed in some of the photographs of Becky the same red mist and an indication that Becky has a special gift. One day I feel Becky will acknowledge her special talent; however, she is a young lady with her life ahead of her, and she did to enjoy her life and gain experience.

27th Dec 06

Jane, Becky, Vicky and I drove to Blackpool to visit Julie (sister of Jane). The Spirits started to touch my face. I asked for the name of the spirit. The name "Michael" came into my mind. Jane said that's her father's name, and when she said this, the spirit touched me again on the face to confirm that it was indeed Michael. I felt he was happy for Jane to go and see her sister. Michael did not provide a message at this stage. We stayed at Julie's house for a couple of hours, then travelled to Jane's mother, who lived in a residential home in Preston. We were talking to Jane's Mum and her auntie Joan. I spirit Michael started touching my face. It seemed he was just showing a presence, but still, no message came through. As we were travelling by car to Rochdale, Jane said her father's girlfriend was also living in the same building as Jane's mother. Spirit Michael again touched my face confirming what Jane had said, but he did not provide a message. This time I said to Michael John Thom to confirm that it was him and touch the right side of my face; this did happen and confirmed that it was him. I then asked him to provide evidence. The word sweets came to mind, followed by Mojo, Jelly babies. I asked Jane who liked Mojo`s chews. Jane said she does, Becky does, and her father like Jelly babies and that he always bit their heads off when he was on the earth plane. I do feel that Michael John Thom is not at rest, he is worried about his family, and he is seeking forgiveness. He wants me to pass a message to his ex-wife (Jane's Mother).

29th Dec 06

I went to Preston to see Jane's Mother. She knew I was a spirit medium, and she agreed to see me. I was invited into her flat by her sister. In a conversation, I told them a spirit named Michael John Thom. They asked for confirmation, Michael mentioned the letters JJJs. I asked what this meant, and they told me that JJJs stands for Joyce, Joan, and Jean. They are all sisters. I then went on to say that there are a lot of problems around the family now. Spirit Michael continued to pass the message to Joyce. He said Joyce needs to sort out the problems before the family breaks up. Spirit Michael said he wanted to be with Joyce for his life on earth. Joyce confirmed this and said they were going to get back together. Michael then said that he was not good at relationships, and he had no favourites in his children. They were all equal to him. Michael brought a lot of memories to Joyce that put a smile on her face, and she confirmed that she still loves him despite what's has happened. Sometimes spirit will impress on you to pass their messages on to someone who really needs help. Always ask before you give the message. You don't want to offend anyone.

30th Dec 06

I meditated in my bedroom and opened with a hymn and a prayer. I started to receive touching sensations around my face. I asked the spirits which they were, and I would like to get to know them all. I was touched on my left temple area, and it felt like an electric spark. I then experienced that the spirits were showering me with water (I felt they were cleaning me). The name "Helen" entered my mind. I asked the spirits to confirm this by touching my left ear. Seconds later, spirit Helen touched my left ear. I was so happy that spirit Helen was with me. I became very emotional and got upset and cried. This was the feeling I had during the light trance state, which lasted for several minutes. Spirit Helen instructed me to visit her son Peter and to tell him not to worry about her. She wanted me to explain to Peter how she feels now she is in the spirit world, and he needs to start living his life and be happy. I had to see the photograph in the kitchen. Helen was a very good friend of mine when she was on the earth, and I used to visit her regularly.

31st Dec 06

I went to visit Peter at his house, in Aston-under-Lyne. I knocked on the kitchen door, and Peter answered. He was very surprised to see me and invited me inside. When I entered, I noticed a picture of his mother Helen above the

Healing Hands on the kitchen wall. That's the photograph Helen had told me about. I explained to Peter what had happened to me the day before and that his mother had come to me and told me to go and see him. I said to Peter about a candlewick bed cover upstairs, and he confirmed this was on his bed and it used to be on his mother's bed. I went on to say that there is a wind-up watch in her bedroom; he confirmed this to be true. My face went cold on the left side, and I told Peter his mother was here with us. I said to Peter she liked a tot of Whisky before bed, and he confirmed this. I then told him that she said tonight, New Year's Eve, have a tot of Whisky at midnight for her. Peter said he would do this. Peter gave me several photographs of her. Helen was a nice lady who took a shine to me. I always showed her respect and helped her when she was very poorly. I remember pushing her around the hospital in her wheelchair and making her laugh. I always found the time to help her no matter what, and I know she loved her son Peter very much. I remember the big smile on her face when I went to see her and give her a big kiss; she enjoyed having all the attention. I will always think of her, and I know she is with me in spirit, and I would not be surprised that she is protecting me and guiding me.

4th Jan 07

Lawrence and I attended Shaw Spiritual Church and found it to be shut. We decided to go to Dearnley Spiritual Church for the open circle. Spirit medium "Paul Hunt" took the service. The open circle was announced, and I addressed the congregation and asked if I could link with the medium. He said yes. I explained to him whilst he was demonstrating, I observed shadows, and I felt touching sensations on my face. I said that he has just got over a bad relationship, and now the pathways are clear for him to go forward and be happy, he confirmed. I mentioned that he is reading a book about spiritualism to increase his knowledge. He smiled and said yes. I went on to say the name "Frank" had something to do with him, but I did not know if Frank was in the spirit or on the earth plane. He confirmed this and held his phone up, and said he was waiting for a call because his friend "Frank" was about to pass over into the spirit world of energies. I said a snake was at his feet, and the spirit handed him a stick. The snake was for him to be on his guard regarding a situation and the Rock was for sweetness. I thanked the spiritual medium for his link and left him with the Love of Spirit.

Mr Paul Hunt approached me and thanked me for my accurate messages for him, and he explained that his friend, Frank, was very ill and it was likely that he would die at any

193

moment. He also confirmed that he is reading spiritual books for further knowledge and that he had just got over a relationship break-up. Paul said it was one of the most accurate messages he has ever had. Always trust your spirit helpers when they are passing messages to you. They will never let you down, and their message will mean something even if you don't.

10th Jan 07

Lawrence and I attended Whitefield Spiritual church for the open circle. Spiritual Medium Doreen Hodgkinson was demonstrating that evening. When the open circle was announced, I got up and addressed the congregation. I asked `Terry`, who was a member of our development class, if I could speak to him. An elderly spirit male named Terry draws close to him; he confirms this. Spirit Terry placed him in a hot bath for relaxation and suggested he needed to calm down and be more approachable. I went on to say that he ignores people when they are moaning at him and that he should listen. Spirit Terry said that he must stop being violent and learn how to have respect for everyone. I thanked him for his link and left him with the Love of Spirit.

I was directed to a couple and asked if I could link with them, and they said yes. I told them that there are Orbs (spirits) around them, and their Christmas has been a quiet affair, and there had been a recent passing. The word mum came through; they both confirmed this.

The spirit mother said; they have to have their Christmas now and be happy because she is safe and well, and she wants to see the children smiling. In further conversation, she said that she is a reserved person, but only until she got to know you. She also said she wanted to see their businesses back on track and become successful. The spirit lady mentioned a Christmas tree and kept repeating this. However, I did not have the opportunity to mention this information.

Terry said the spirit male was his father, and lately, he has been nervous, and he said he is trying to relax.

The couple confirmed that the spirit lady was their mother who had recently passed to the spirit world. I did not mention they still had their Christmas tree. However, the couple told me that they still have the Christmas tree up in the front room in respect of their mother's passing over.

11th Jan 2007

Lawrence, Tracy, Julie and I attended Dewsbury Spiritual Church for the open circle. In this circle, if anyone had a message, then they could use this time to speak. I addressed the sitters and provided an Inspirational talk about "Our Sixth Sense", followed by a message. I asked the

195

audience who had a hole in their sock. Nobody answered this. I knew that someone close by had a hole in their sock. I was directed to a female and asked if I could create a link with her. She said yes. I described a spirit male energy to her, and he wore a very tight belt for support. She confirmed this. I then went to say that he wants her to know that he is with her and guiding her. I left her with the love of spirit.

I spoke to another sitter in the circle and mentioned two names to her; she confirmed the two spirits. I informed her there was a spirit boy who had recently died, and he gave her a dandelion flower. She confirmed this and explained it was good evidence because the little boy thought all flowers were dandelions.

I was drawn to a young man and said that a spirit male energy was with me, and I described him to the chap. The young male confirmed this spirit male. I asked if I could create a link with him, and he agreed. I went on to say that his spirit grandfather was happy to see him at a spiritual centre. His spirit grandfather was happy to be able to communicate with him. He then mentioned when he was on the earth. He did not believe in the afterlife. I mentioned the sock with a hole, and he confirmed this by showing the sock. I told him that he would progress in his spiritual beliefs, and he is to read spiritual books, which would answer his questions and provide him with knowledge. I left him with the love of spirit.

It does not matter if no one can understand your spirit messages, sometimes people do not want to speak in front of crowds, or they are shy. Eventually, the person for who the message is for will no doubt speak to you privately. Never take a no from people personally. Believe in your spirit communicators. They will never let you down. We sometimes get the message wrong because of our own interpretation. It is important not to add to the spiritual message just for glamorising.

13th Jan 07

Lawrence and I went to Blackpool Spiritual Church for the Open Circle. Lawrence addressed the open circle with some remarkable evidence, and once he sat down. I got up and addressed the open circle. I was drawn to an elderly female and asked if I could link with her. She said yes. I said I have two female spirits energies with me, 'Nora' and Molly`, this lady confirmed these names. These spirit ladies mentioned that a male had recently passed over to the spirit world of energies.

The lady told me it was her husband who passed over a couple of weeks ago. I then went on to say that the three of them were playing the game Hop, skip and jump, and her husband was cheating. This lady laughed and said that would be him. I mentioned she had something to do with dominos, and she confirmed this by saying her grandson was teaching her last week how to play. I then said her husband was with her, watching and helping her. Furthermore, there was evidence of a teddy bear she had got, and she confirmed this by telling me that her friend had just bought her one. I said that a member of the family who is in spirit had an allotment to grow fruit and vegetables and that she should eat well and that she is unsteady on her feet. This lady confirmed this. I thanked her for her link and left her with the Love of Spirits

17th Jan 2007

Lawrence and I attended Whitefield Spiritual Church for the open circle. The spirit medium seemed to be very nervous and quiet speaking, but he did great work and provided some good evidence. When the open circle was announced, `Doreen` asked me to address the congregation. I stood up and asked to link with a male member. He said yes. I provided a name and description of female spirit energy and offered it to the male. He replied "NO" twice. I then presented the evidence to the congregation. A female could relate to the name and description of the female spirit. I thanked the male for his link. The female said she knew the female spirit. At this point, there were spirit lights (orbs) around her and another young female, which indicated the message was for both. I spoke to her daughter and provided evidence about her lifestyle and her type of humour. Spirit mentioned she was at present unhappy. This young lady confirmed this. I thanked her for her link and left her with the Love of Spirit.

This evening was very hard for me to work on behalf of the spiritual energies. At one stage, I thought I was guessing, and that was the last thing I wanted to do. It shows you; you have to be prepared to work, and for some reason, there could be weak energy in the building, which will make it hard for the spirit to build up energy. Furthermore, you cannot get complacent and sometimes spirit will test you, and I certainly felt I was being tested.

18th Jan 2007

I arrived at Quarmby Spiritual Church, Huddersfield, Yorkshire, for the open circle. The spirit male medium started with philosophy, which was moving, and he demonstrated by using coloured Sand. When the service started, I received a touching sensation on my face. The open circle started with different spirit mediums speaking. I seemed to be drawn to a female. However, I felt that I did not have a message for her from the spirit. I did not present myself on this occasion. I believe that I was not meant to work that evening, so I did not push it. I thought it was best to relax and enjoy the service.

20th Jan 2007

I was on my bed, relaxing, and after a short time, my mind's eyes opened. It started with violet-coloured dots, which grew langer in size, similar to a T.V screen. I was looking into a modern room with electrics and asked if anyone was there. I received no answer to my question. Then I was on the landing of the house, and a female spirit with slim short dark hair, wearing black underwear, walked to the bathroom. I observed a spirit male entering the shower in the main bedroom where the female spirit had been. I got a glass of cold water and went into the main bedroom and threw it over the spirit male for a joke, and quickly walked out so he would not know who had thrown the cold water. The spirit female was now in the bath, relaxing. I walked down the stairs. At this point, I came out of my meditation state. This was a strange happening. I believe this was meant for someone in the future, or I was being made aware of this about to happen.

Sometimes we do find it difficult to try and piece together the information being sent. It shows that there is still a lot to learn about spirit events.

24th Jan 2007

Lawrence and I went to Sowerby Bridge Spiritual Church for the open circle. There was no spirit medium, and anyone who had a message could speak. As I sat there listening to the speaker, I felt that the energies of the spirit were not around me this evening. Two ladies provided a message for me. Near the end of the service, a female speaker said to me I must speak and trust the spirits, and I am at a crossroads and don't know which way to turn. She then went on to say that I am very well blessed with a spirit link. The lady then sat down. I address the open circle with philosophy titled "Spiritual" and mentioned don't prejudge. I then said to the president that there used to be Morris Dancer in this building. The message was not for her, but it had something to do with the church. She thanked me for making her aware of that.

I then asked the open circle if anyone could take the named spirit Dennis, several hands went up. I then said Dennis liked cowboy & Indian films when he was on the Earth Plane. One lady confirmed this. I thank the rest of the sitters for their help.

I asked the lady if I could work with her, and she replied yes. I went on to say that she could not make her mind up if she received a message from spirit, and she questions this all the time. She confirmed this, I told her there is a Native American with her, and he is guiding her on her spiritual journey, and when she gets a message from the spirit guide, no matter what the message is about, she must try and pass this message on. The message will mean something to that person. Furthermore, I said she experiences tingling sensations all over her body, and she confirmed this with a smile on her face. For me, this is an indication of spiritual healing energies. I left her with the Love of Spirit.

I was then drawn to a male and said, you are a fit man, and gave him advice regarding training. He could not take this, but I knew I was with him because I had seen a shadow of a head of a spirited person on the carpet in front of me. I then said you know a Dennis also, he said No, and his mannerism was clear that he was now blocking me. I mentally asked spirit for further evidence. I said to the male the words, Dennis the Menace. This was you in your earlier years. He laughed and confirmed by saying, weren't we all? I said I was not here to question that. I then provided further evidence, which he accepted. The president was indicating for me to finish, which put me off track. I left him with the Love of Spirit.

Sometimes you will come across people who like to be blockers, people who come for a reason other than being friendly. Maybe they have doubts, and that is their choice.

You have to always be polite and stern. Never let sceptic trouble you.

27th Jan 2007

Lawrence and I went to Saddleworth Spiritual Church for the opening circle. The female spirit medium did her philosophy in a soft, relaxed tone which made you feel relaxed. The open circle was announced. I stood up and addressed the congregation with a philosophy titled, "follow your instincts." I had a direct link to a female and said to her, "You could take the philosophy, couldn't you?" She replied yes. I then went on to say that she is being torn between two parties about a situation, and she does not know which way to turn, she agreed. Furthermore, I told her she had a major decision to make regarding her children. She confirmed this. I then described male spirit energy to her, and she knew this male; she smiled. I told her this spirit male energy was her father. She replied yes. Her spirit father said to stop being too soft with people because they will only continue to take from you, and she must follow her instincts. The lady after the service told me that the message I provided for her was correct and she felt inspired to follow through her the decision, which has been difficult for her. She has been very worried and upset, now she is happy and thanked me for the message which has been a big help to her.

30th Jan 2007

A female who had found Monty on New Year's Eve knocked at my front door. I opened the door, and she stood there crying and upset. I invited her inside and made her a cup of tea. She told me that she had just been told some bad news regarding her lover, who had been rushed into hospital because he had a heart attack, and that she could not go to see him because of his family and wife. She then said to me about her work situation. I started to see small shadows around her and small coloured lights. Then I said to her do you know Julie on the earth plane. She said yes then asked why. I told her that she needed to tell Julie that things would work out in the end for the better. I then described an elderly spirit male energy and said it was her father and that he has been with trying to make her aware he is around her. She said she was aware of him in the night. I confirmed that her situation would become positive.

I then went on to say that she would be going to Sweden in the next couple of months and that her ex-husband was going to say sorry to her for the way he treated her. I mentioned that a spirit male energy named Harry was next to her, and she confirmed that she knew Harry. I said that all her spirit loved ones are with her all the time, looking and guiding her.

I feel she had been sent to my house so her spirit loved ones could communicate with her. This lady offered me money for providing a spirit message for her, but I refused and said, you looked after Monty when he went missing, and you needed help from spirit. That's why they came through. She left with a smile on her face.

It is amazing how spirit can influence us by creating situations around us, and we instantly follow their guide without realising it.

31st Jan 2007

Lawrence and I went to Sowerby Bridge Spiritual Church for the open circle. Several people got up and gave messages. I tried on three occasions to try and speak, but each time someone beat me to it. Near the end of the service, I had the chance to stand up. I addressed the Open Service. I described a male in the spirit world, and a female in the audience said she knows the spirited male, I asked her if I could link with her, and she said yes. I informed her that there was a slight unbalance in her family, she confirmed this. I then went on to say that a Unicorn was directing her along her pathway for guidance, and she must go forward and not be distracted.

I then had the chance to link with a male who said I could work with him. I described a male in the spirit world, and he confirmed this. Also, I mentioned Henry, again he confirmed this. I then said that he needed to relax and that he must make an important decision. He confirmed this to be true. I then went on to say problems, and difficult situations come, and he dismissed them in an instant and continued that he knew a gentleman named Tom on the earth plane, he agreed. Tom would guide him on his spiritual journey, and that is all I have to say to him. The male looked at me and nodded.

I provided a message for a male when I was at Sowerby Bridge on 24th Jan 2007. This male came up to me and said what I had said about a Dennis came true, and he thanked me for that. Sometimes spirit can provide a name which would be for two people. If they can save energy, they will. It goes to show some people's mannerisms are not what they seem.

4th Feb 2007

I attended Dearnley Spiritual Church for the Divine Service. The female spirit medium demonstrated her clairvoyance, and at the same time, I noticed the colour orange over my right knee. After a brief period, the colour moved to my left knee. I had injured my knees whilst serving in the British Army, and I was medically discharged in 1990. I relate to the colour orange as an illness or injury. If I see it on a person, I know there is some sort of medical condition in that area.

I am also aware that my development has turned to another level, this being indicated by the human aura and colours. Each colour has its own vibration, which, in my opinion, is part of energy.

6th Feb 2007

Tracy, my friend, came around to my house for lunch as we chatted. I informed Tracy there was something of sentimental value in her house, like a painting, and it was in the attic. She replied that she had just found an old picture in the attic of a Russian Family. She then went on to say she would try and find some information regarding the painting.

Spirits will try to contact you at anytime, anyplace; therefore, it is essential to keep control and only create a link when you are ready. You have a life in the physical world.

7th Feb 2007

Lawrence Simms and I went to Whitefield Spiritual Church for the open circle service. Doreen, our development teacher, was chairing the service, and she announced the open circle. I addressed the small congregation with a philosophy about vibrations and explained the different ways our spirit loved ones communicate, and our spirit loved ones and friends are always around us. A spirit elderly female of 5` 4" tall, medium build, long dark hair in a ponytail wanted to speak to a female in the audience, I asked her if we could speak with her, and she replied yes. I informed the female that it was her spirit grandmother communicating, and she was saying she was still not listening to her inner thoughts and that she should listen to her intuition. She confirmed this. I went on to say the name, "Elizabeth", and there was a mention of hospital conditions. She again understood this message. Further evidence was provided from spirit about the female having family near the river Mersey and North Wales and that she stayed in a caravan a few times with her family. This lady was happy to receive a message from her spirit family. I thank her for her link.

Doreen informed me that spirits were slowing me down by placing a stopper in front of me. She went on to say I had an important decision to make, and spirit has placed a helmet on my head for protection.

I did not understand this, but I listened and waited to see what it meant in due course. Slow down, I thought. If I was slow, I would move backwards.

8th Feb 07

I was painting the fence at my house and at the same time relaxed my mind and sent out my thoughts to the spirit world.

I received a thought back telling me to slow down and use the painting as an example. If we take our time, we all get there in the end, and if we rush, we will miss things on the way. Well, that told me, it is amazing when you think you are doing well. You are never too late to listen at all times regarding your inner mind.

14th Feb 07

Lawrence and I went to Ashton-under-Lyne Spiritual Church for the open circle service. When the open circle was announced, several persons demonstrated their gifts. Towards the end, I addressed the congregation and asked if I could speak to the male spirit medium on the platform. He said yes. I describe an Indian male wearing a turban was with him and what appeared to be a monk. The spirit medium named Robert confirmed this. Furthermore, I said that he was a musical person and that he plays the guitar in a band. I said to him the Indian and the Monk said he has to write down everything that enters his mind, and he will find it the words will be a song from the spirit, and he should sing and play on stage, and this will be his philosophy. I observed a large shadow on the wall behind the medium; it appeared this was a shadow of a male. Figure three came into my mind, and I asked the spirit medium if he could relate to the number three. He said no. I asked him whether he would remember what I had said because number three has something to do with him, and it is a meaning for him.

An elderly female in the church was sitting on her own, I asked if I could speak to her, and she said yes. I told her that a spirit male energy was sitting beside her throughout the service and described him as 5'10 tall, slim build, smartly dressed and sitting with an upright posture. I said it was her husband, and she said yes and smiled. I went on to say he placed his arm around her for comfort, and at times she felt down and sad.

The simplest message can bring comfort to someone who is missing their loved one who had died recently. So never hold back; you are here to help.

20th Feb 2007

I was at Whitefield Spiritual Church and observed at the right of the rostrum clouds and several spirit faces; they kept on coming and going showing different faces. I asked them could they be clearer, but they did not. However, this lasted for several minutes (20min). When the service was closing, and we were saying our prayers, I felt several spirits touching my face, to the point it tickled me. I nearly laughed. My friend Lawrence Simms was on the platform working, I observed a square-shaped orange colour to the right side of him on the wall, and a thought entered my mind regarding Lawrence. I sensed he had some sort of medical troubles.

Upon my bed reading my book, I felt touching sensations on my body. I closed my eyes and meditated. Seconds later, I heard a noise, as if someone was throwing stones up at the window, and a voice shouted my name, David. I looked out of the window, and the street was empty. Monty did not bark or give any signs of someone near the house. The noise and voice were very clear, as if I heard it with my physical ears, when in fact, I heard it in my mind. We can easily become confused when a spirit's audible communication comes. Remember, spirits work with a faster vibration than the earth. Your physical senses for the ear are of the earth's vibration.

21st Feb 2007

Lawrence and I went to Whitefield Spiritual Church for the open circle. After the service, the open circle was announced. I addressed the audience and explained to a female whose child was in a pram. I observed small lights around the child, and she was pointing to them. (Spirit orbs). I then said to her spirit within is trying to make her smile cause at the moment, she has low self-esteem, and she is finding things difficult. This lady confirmed. I then went on to say she likes slapstick comedy and reminded her that she laughed at someone tripping in the last few days. She laughed and said yes. I told her that the spirits had placed a jester hat on her head for fun times.

As the child was in the pram, she kept looking towards me and pointing, and when her mother let her out of the pram. This child came straight over to me to play and show me things. As the service continued, the child kept on talking and trying to draw my attention. It seems we both had a link between us for some reason, and all the time, the child had a huge smile on her face. Children are more susceptible to spirit communication because of their innocents, and I feel spirit was letting me know that the child was aware of spirits in the room.

28th Feb 2007

I went to Whitefield Spiritual church for the open circle. Doreen was sat next to me, and Peter Clarke was chairing the service. When the open circle was announced, I got up and addressed the congregation. I said that someone in this church had a hole in their sock. They all looked at me with surprised looks. A female said she had a hole in her pop sock. I asked if I could work with her, she agreed. I then described a spirit male energy and mentioned he had tattoos on his arms, and he was a middle-aged man. She confirmed this description. I went on to say that sometimes he was abrupt, and I said the name was Frank. She confirmed this to be true. In the further conversation, I said about a difficult situation that was worrying her and told her things were going to get better. I then said that she talks to herself when she is ironing, and that spirit Frank listens to her. She laughed and said yes. She chats to herself all the time, especially when she is ironing. But is she speaking to herself?

1st Mar 2007

Lawrence and I went to Dearnley Spiritual Church for the open circle. For the first time in a while, the atmosphere was good, and the spirit medium Les Gardner provided a great service. When the open circle was announced, I stood up and addressed the congregation and asked a female if I could work with her. She replied yes. I described female spirit energy to her and provided her name of "Ann or Annie". She confirmed this to be right. I then told her that there were two Ann's, one in spirit and one on the earth plane. She could not place Ann on the earth plane. I said could she watch out for the name, `Ann`, on the earth plane. I then described to her her life situation and explained it was going to get much better, but we must be patient.

I was drawn to another female and asked if I could speak to her. She said yes. Quickly, I said that she was worried about a situation with her family. She confirmed this, I told her things were going to get better, and spirit had placed a condition on me, a sore throat. She confirmed this and said that the person she is worried about has a sore throat.

I enjoy passing messages on in the open circles because there is no pressure, and it usually is one or two messages you can provide.

5th Mar 2007

Doreen and I went to Hebden Bridge Spiritual Church. Doreen was taking the Divine Service and asked me if I wanted to join her on the platform. I said yes. Doreen asked me would I like to do the philosophy, and I accepted. This was a proud moment for me. The philosophy lasted for twenty minutes. I addressed the congregation and asked to speak to a male. He said yes. I explained about his life situation and that he had to make an important decision, he replied yes. I then said that his life now has been a struggle, and he is about to enter calm waters. This male understood what was being said by spirits. I told him I have a Unicorn with him, and symbolically means, for direction, go straight forward. The colour yellow and blue was being shown around the male. Yellow is for intelligence and blue for spiritual thoughts.

Doreen then gave me the opportunity to address the congregation again, I asked to speak to a lady, and she said yes. I told her there was something about a fire and could she take this. She said no, not now. I then said that a spirit male energy was with me, and he shouted that he did not mean to start the fire and that he was sorry. She then said she remembered a fire a few years ago. I asked her to take it and would she look for further information within her family. I went on to mention female spirit energy, 5'6" tall slim build and very attractive, the recipient confirmed. I passed on the message to the recipient, and she understood exactly what the message meant.

There was an indication the female recipient had psychic qualities. Sometimes the message can come in a symbolic method, and you need to find the meaning.

6th Mar 07

I started my meditation with a prayer for my friend Andrea, whose family are part of the native American Indians, 'Cherokee.' After the prayer, I relaxed my mind and body. Moments later, my mind's eye opened, and I observed a violet-coloured dot, which expanded to the width of my view. Like a television screen, the violet remained around the edges. Sat there looking at me was a Chinese male spirit with long thin hair, long thin goatee beard and wearing what appeared to be a Black Satin Chinese Shirt with buttons down the front. I said hello. He continued looking at me, and as he faded away. The word "Tolu" entered my mind. Several spirit faces were now looking at me. It seemed they were curious about my presence. These spirit people's energies looked like they came from a professional background when they were on the earth. At this point, I became aware of my surroundings. Research for the word "Tolu", which means - fragrant gum obtained from the bark of a leguminous South American tree used in cough mixtures, flavourings, perfumes.

I did not understand why they introduced the word 'Tolu,' at the time. It could have been an indication of spiritual healing.

7th Mar 2007

Lawrence Simms and I went to Whitefield Spiritual Church for the open circle. The open circle was announced, and I addressed the audience. I said when you have a moment on your own, and you sing, this means you're happy, everyone agreed. I mentioned there is a person here in the audience who sings when they are on their own. A lady put her hand up and said she does a lot of singing when no one is around. I asked if I could speak to her, she agreed. I mentioned a song titled "I WILL SURVIVE" and the name "Sharon", she confirmed this. I said I was being made aware of a problem around this lady Sharon, who needed help.

216

I then said I had a spirit male named 'Tom' with me. She said she did not understand the name, Tom. I asked her to take the name and check her family tree, she agreed. I then again went on to say she gets on with everybody and likes to have a laugh and be happy. I then mentioned horses; she said yes. I told her I had her on a horse with a lance charging people. She laughed and said yeah. I told her that she was spiritually aware and that she heard and saw the spirit, and when she told her friends, they all laughed at her. She said yes, they do! I told her I had her in a bath with oils and yellow ducks and toys, she laughed, and everyone laughed.

After the service had finished, the lady who I had spoken to said her sister had the yellow ducks in her bath. She went on to say thank you for the message and that it was very accurate.

I thanked the lady and told her it was spirit energies she was thanking. I am the link between both worlds.

8th Mar 2007

Lawrence Simms and I went to Quarmby Spiritual Church, Huddersfield, for the open circle service. The open circle was started, and several psychics demonstrated and passed on messages. I addressed the open circle and mentioned a spirit male energy draws close to me with his hands in his pocket and shaking coins. I described the male

217

spirit energy to the open circle. A female put her hand up and said she knew this spirit male. I informed her that the spirit male was a jovial sort of chap, who likes comedy, and he liked Charlie Chaplin, Laurel & Hardy. She smiled and said yes, yes. I went on to say that he is aware of her being at a low ebb lately, and he is trying to put a smile on her face and then mentioned she is trying to get something or reaching out. Every time she gets close, it seems to get further away. She understood what this message meant. I said that one day she would achieve her objective and not give up. I mentioned a green plant, she laughed and said yes. Furthermore, I said she is spiritually aware. I told her she drives her car to work using the same route every day. She confirmed this. I went on to say she should change her route and drive slower than she is now. Just before the service had finished, I was summoned again by spirits to address the open circle.

I explained that spirits energies liked to see smiling faces and happy people, which would create strong energy so they can come forward. I said I didn't think of one person, just send out your loving thoughts to the spirit world of energies. I also mentioned you would be surprised who passes on messages, which could be from a family, friends, neighbours, or it could be a message for someone else. I went on to say if you cannot relate to a message from spirit, take it with you and do your research. This is the best evidence you can receive. I then explained by folding your arms and legs, you close the chakras, and this blocks out spirits and makes it hard for them to communicate.

I said someone in the open circle must decide, and they are unsure what the answer would be. I explained you must follow your instincts, your first thought. Many people don't listen to their inner thoughts and usually make the wrong decision. The first thought that enters your mind will come from the spirit world of energies, so follow your instincts and act.

Everyone has a choice about their life situations. You decide what is best for you and not let others do it for you. Their decision might not suit you because it comes from their mind. That's why you should think first before you decide. When do you think you are automatically analysing your decision?

If we follow the pathway of the Godhead, then we are following God's Love for everyone and everything. You must learn how to love unconditionally, be respectful and learn to forgive. If you cannot forgive, how can you love?

The doors to the building should always be open to anyone, and they should be made welcome. God does not judge, so why should we?

You cannot take material things with you when you pass over to the world of spirit, so it does not matter what you have in the material of value. In the spirit world, everyone is equal. There is no person better than any other person. Remember, if you must decide, make the decision and be proud of taking control of your life.

I felt inspired to conduct some philosophy for the audience, and it showed on their concentration that they enjoyed what was mentioned. So you see, spirit energies work in many different ways to get their message over.

11th Mar 2007

The Divine Service at Whitefield Spiritual Church was conducted by Doreen Hodkinson's development class, and this was named `Fledging Service`. There was seven fledging named: Janet, Lawrence, Steven, Vicky, Julie, Peter and me. We all had ten minutes to demonstrate and provide a message for the congregation. Janet opened the service with a prayer, which was followed by a hymn. Doreen, who conducted the chair, announced the service to start. David (me) started off with philosophy explaining about people find themselves rushing around from one place to another in body and mind. I then was directed to a lady by spirit energy and said the philosophy was for her. She said yes and understood. I asked her if I could work with her, and she replied yes. I then went on to say I have a spirit male energy wearing a donkey jacket, and he was some sort of engineer when on the earth plane, and they were several other spirit people wearing boiler suits with him. She confirmed and said it was her husband. I then went on to say that there was a rainbow over her and the two ladies who were sitting next to her. She said they were family. In further conversation, he mentioned there was a recent passing, and their last Christmas was not a happy one. She confirmed this. Furthermore, I told them the message is that things are going to be happier for them in the next few months, and I can see calmer waters ahead.

I then said that someone in the family is thinking of going abroad for Christmas and they should go. She confirmed this. The spirits relayed another message, and I said someone who is an animal lover, and there is a fox which has something to do with them. She smiled and said a fox goes to her husband's grave, and she feeds the fox. She also said she has a fox ornament next to her fireplace. I left them with their love of the spirit and thanked them for their contact.

At the end of the service, Doreen asked me to do the closing prayer, followed by a hymn. The congregation was so pleased with all the fledging they all started to clap. Doreen was very proud of her students. It is important to follow your teacher's advice when demonstrating in public. It is crucial to start demonstrating alongside an experience development class teacher. If you struggle, your teacher can help you by supplying energy and explaining how to deliver your message.

13th Mar 07

I attended our development class at Whitefield Spiritual Church, taken by our teacher Doreen Hodkinson. They are twelve students in the class, and they are as follows: Peter 1, Peter 2, Julie 1, Julie 2, Janet, Patrick, Tony, Steve, Terry, Vicky, Avril, and myself. Doreen selected one of us to start with an opening prayer and then followed by ten minutes of meditation to selected music. We then, in turn, on the command of Doreen, stand on the rostrum to demonstrate to the remaining students. At the same time, Doreen's spirit teachers and helpers work with her. Doreen makes sure that we present ourselves in a professional manner, and we must address the congregation with precise wording.

Doreen explained that when working on the rostrum at Spiritualist Churches, we must be dressed in suitable clothing, and she teaches us the wording we can and cannot say. I stood on the rostrum and addressed my fellow students by saying, "Good evening, my friends", followed by philosophy on the subject "Jealousy." I explained the word

'Jealousy can make someone do and say things they do not mean; it changes their personality. Not many people will accept they are too jealous of another person, but it will eventually reveal itself.

We can help those victims who have been subjected to mental torture because of someone who is jealous of them. They can have a low opinion of themselves, or they can lose their self-esteem and confidence. I have found people who are jealous of others lack confidence, and they have a low ebb.

I finished the brief philosophy and asked to speak to Julie. She agreed. I mentioned to her that her psychic abilities were becoming stronger, as indicated by the spirit energies. I feel this message came from a spirit male energy which was 6'1" tall, slim build, grey brushed-back hair, and with smoke stains on his fingers.

Doreen said to ask for a name! I asked for a name and the word "Doug or Douglas". Julie could not take this at the time. Julie's mother then said she remembered Doug and told Julie she then remembered Doug. Doreen then asked if I could investigate her family tree and find him. I then went on to say that she should watch for a near collision whilst she drove her vehicle. She should change her route to work. I also said that the number ten means something to her or it

223

will mean something. Julie could not take this. I asked her to watch out for it and left her with the love of spirit. I felt awful, this was the first time I had not had it easy from spirits energies, and I feel it was my own fault. I did have a conversation with Lawrence before we entered the development class that I was going to try and get things wrong. That was a Big Mistake!

I feel spirits taught me a valuable lesson, and that was not to be complacent and to always seek evidence. You cannot tell spirit how you will work; they will decide what type of communication when demonstrating. When you are in the development class, work to the best of your ability.

14th Mar 2007

Lawrence and I attended Sowerby Bridge Spiritual Church for the open circle. When the open circle was announced, I addressed the open circle and offered the name Eric and that he was an engineer. Five people put their hands up. I then narrowed it down to a female and asked if I could work with her. I told her the description of the male, and she said she did not understand. I asked for further evidence, and the spirit energies said that she had an argument with a friend, she confirmed. I explained that don't argue back because it makes the situation worse, and it is harder to walk away, but you must, and you will benefit in the long run. I then said she was unsure about a decision; she did not understand. I then said that she had been feeling low and the spirit of Eric would not open it any further. She said no. This lady did say she had anxiety. I then went on to say to her she watches DVDs film she said no. seconds later, she said that she works in a video shop selling DVDs. I thanked her for her time.

It became clear to me this lady was blocking me for some reason, and the lesson learnt is that she kept asking the spirit for more evidence because she was not saying no to my personality; she was saying no to spirit for every reason she may have. Lawrence Simms addressed the congregation and provided evidence for three females. Lawrence provided further evidence, and they all said no. He then asked for more information from spirit and relayed it to the ladies again. They all said no. Lawrence then went on to say that female spirit energy was throwing away shoes. Still, the ladies claimed they did not understand.

Lawrence then said that he could see the female spirit throwing away the shoes. One of the females said the female spirit had no legs, and she knew this female spirit. Lawrence said that's why she is throwing away the shoes. He then provided further evidence, and again all three ladies said no. Lawrence then thanked them for their time and left them.

I addressed the open circle and mentioned about people sat with their legs and arms folded, and this would make it difficult for the spirit medium to work with them. Furthermore, I said that spirits like to see smiling faces, just like when you are at work you like to see smiling faces. I was drawn to a female and said to her can I work with her. She said yes.

I told her I have a spirit male energy with me wearing a scholar's hat, a professor type of person, and he has told me she is studying. She confirmed this. I went on to say that she is studying a course with something to do with "Arthur Findley College", Stanstead Hall. She again confirmed. I mentioned spirits are saying do not give up you will achieve your aim. Spirit confirmed this by saying she has or is going to Stanstead Hall. She replied she had just returned. I then went on to say the spirit professor is helping her. I said thank you for your contact.

I then asked another female if I could work with her, and she said yes. I told her at this present time, nobody understands her, she confirmed this. I went on to say she is being a victim of a jealousy campaign. She confirmed this. I mentioned she loves animals, and there is a silver wolf next to her providing protection from negative thoughts and an Eagle which has sharp eyes sight.

This Eagle is symbolic for her to see clearly about situations around her. She confirmed this. I then mentioned spirits are making me aware of cats, and they are a comfort to her. I then told her that situations were on the up, and she would feel comfortable in the next few months, and she would over gain her confidence. She thanked me, and I ended the conversation.

Sometimes when you visit certain Spiritualist Churches, you may find that the member will make it difficult for you to work with spirits. This could be for many reasons, and I feel this was another spirit test to see if you will not be perturbed and carry on with your messages. Not all people want a message from the spirit world. They are just happy to watch and listen to other people's messages. A lot of people do not like speaking in the open, and some people get embarrassed.

There are many factors that can make it difficult for a spirit to impress its message on you. However, never give up and trust the spirits. The most important lesson that I learned was to keep on working with the spirits, and eventually, they will provide evidence the recipient cannot refuse. I feel it is better to experience these situations in developing rather than working off a stage or platform. This is one of the reasons why you should not rush your development.

20th Mar 2007

I went to Whitefield Spiritual Church for our development class taken by Doreen Hodkinson. Just as we were about to commence, Doreen informed me, I was the first person to start off the rostrum. I addressed the class with the opening prayer, followed by ten minutes of meditation. I commenced with a philosophy about something that had happened to me during the past week, and I had to learn how to control my anger. I started to explain to the class that when someone whom you have helped through their difficult times, to the extent you have put them first and at the time they were thankful and said they would return the kindness when they are in a better position in life. However, they let you down and leave you in a negative situation.

We must learn not to get angry with them; why? Cause it will only make the problem worse and create more negative thoughts, which thoughts or energy. You can be disappointed with them; don't let anger get the better of you. Don't fight anger with anger; this is one reason why we have wars.

If we all work together and learn how to control our anger and change anger for love compassion, we are helping to create a better world for our children and make the world a safer place.

I then asked a female if I could work with her, and she said yes. I described a spirit lady and provided the name 'Jane and Tracy;' she said she could take those names. I then went on to say that she needs to slow down with her life because she is running around from one point to the next. She confirmed this. I said she is all work and no time for pleasure. She needs to balance the work and pleasure to get an even medium, and when she is serving customers, she sometimes talks under her breath. She smiled and said yes. I then went on to say she has a strong spiritual connection and spirits take her to the next level, but she needs to relax before she starts the development class and keeps all her negative thoughts at the door, and she will find spirits will be able to impress themselves better with a clear mind. I then confirmed that she is having a conversation with someone (boyfriend), and she needs to go with her thoughts because it is right for her. I then finished off by saying to her that she needs to slow down with her driving and stop speeding; she laughed and said yes, she needs to.

21st Mar 2007

Lawrence and I went to Sowerby Bridge Spiritual Church for the open circle. The open circle was announced, and Lawrence addressed the circle and provided some remarkable evidence for an elderly lady who had a huge smile on her face. Lawrence brought laughter into the church. This created the right condition for the spirit to relay messages to the recipients.

I address the open circle with brief philosophy on; "Happiness and Smiling". I asked a lady if I could speak to her, and she replied yes. I asked her if she could take the name 'Caroline' and describe an elderly figure to her, and she said she could take the description but not the name. I said, can she also take a 'Pauline,' she said no. I asked her whether she would search for these names in her family tree. I mentioned to her that I am being made aware of her being slightly down over these past few months. However, better times are coming for her. She confirmed this. I went on to say she used to play a game named hopscotch and swing with a rope with three female friends, and one of her friends would pull the rope to stop it swinging. She laughed and said yes. The elderly spirit female I mentioned was her grandmother, and she used a yellow stone to clean her doorstep, and she confirmed. I informed the lady a female spirit drew close and said the name 'Connie' and asked her if she knew this spirit lady. She confirmed and smiled. Spirit Connie is talking about a situation where someone is angry because they have been let down by them. She confirmed and said it was her who was angry with a person.

I said, 'Connie' would like you to be happy and not fight anger with anger; it only creates bad energies, which will have a knock-on effect. Be happy and smile as you walk down the street.

10th Apr 2007

I went to Whitefield Spiritual Church for my development class with my friend Lawrence Simms. After our meditation, each member of the class had to provide fifteen minutes on the rostrum. I addressed the class and said to Peter Clarke I have no link with spirit. At the same time, the word 'patience' entered my mind. I mentioned an experience that happened to me recently.

As I was talking, I felt a shift in energy around me and was aware of spirits. The names 'Victoria and George' entered my mind, and I offered this to the class members. Peter said yes, he knew these names. Spirit provided further evidence regarding snowflakes in a jar. Peter understood the snowflakes in a glass jar, which was in his house. I then went on to say I had been presented with four rings, he confirmed. I said can you take an Audi motor vehicle he said yes, and he was looking at Audi cars today.

I mentioned a blue convertible, he smiled and said yes. I mentioned a fairground, and he said yes and that he had memories of a fairground where he lives. Furthermore, I said golf driving range, and he said yes and that near his house, he has been on the driving range. I described a male in Sprit who was a jovial chap and the name Norman Wisdom. He said yes, and that he liked Norman Wisdom, I said this was for humour and mentioned Laurel and hardy. Peter said that he had done a crossword, and one of the answers to a question was Laurel and Hardy.

I mentioned the number twelve, Peter said nearly. I went on to say I cannot take it away because the number relates to a boy who is having problems, he confirmed. I told him that he needed to guide the boy because he was always in trouble. I then mentioned a crystal ball. He said that he had one at home. I thanked him for his link and left him with the love of spirit.

12th April 2007

I attended Whitefield Spiritual Church for the open circle. During the service, everybody was concentrating on a huge bee, which was flying around in the church. People became nervous about the bee, and the female spirit medium kept stopping her messages. I lady knocked the bee to the ground, and before I could pick the bee up, a male stood on it and killed it.

We should not kill creatures; they are part of the divine plan. I said a silent prayer for the bee and the male who killed the bee. When the open circle was announced, I was asked to address the open circle. I stated I did not have a link at this time. My friend Janet, who is a wonderful spirit medium, addressed the open circle and relayed a message from spirit with information. As I sat there listening to other mediums speaking, I received a message from a lady. I again was asked if I would address the open circle, and I stood up and introduced myself.

I asked if I could speak to the lady for whom I had a message, she said yes. I told her a spirit male draws close and he has a similar build to myself and provided the name "George" she confirmed she knew this spirit male. Another name was presented to me from spirit; "Norman," again she confirmed. I went on to say she had hurt her hand recently, she replied, she had hurt her hand today. Furthermore, I said she likes Frank Spencer and Charlie Chaplin, and I feel this is for humor because, of late, she has been unhappy, and she confirmed. I mentioned the name, "Mackey," she said yes. I carried on and said can you take the song titled "Simply the Best." This lady told me it's a special song to her because her friend, who is in spirit, played this song and she adored "Tina Turner." I then mentioned a special child who sees and hears spirit. She confirmed this to be her granddaughter. I explained this child has special qualities, and she should listen to her because she is very knowledgeable. I mentioned Dandelion flowers and asked if she understood this evidence. She laughed and said yes, she was pulling them

233

out of the garden today, and she was cursing them. I told her that was spirit confirmation about her granddaughter. I left her with the love of spirit and a bunch of Dandelions.

17th April 2007

Lawrence and I went to Whitefield Spiritual Church for our Development class. I addressed the class and started with brief philosophy about life situations and different types of religions. At the end of the philosophy, I commenced linking to the spirit energies.

I gave a description of a spirit male who was with me. He was 5'8" tall, medium build, and wearing dark trousers supported by a black belt and braces, a white collarless shirt, and holding a tobacco tin. The name "Tom" entered my mind. I offered this to the class, and one of the students confirmed this. I then asked if I could link with her, she replied yes. I mentioned a spirit named "Paul"; she could place him but was not too sure where. I then went on to say a child is revising for an exam soon, she confirmed. Furthermore, I said that she needs to concentrate on her studies which she is not, she confirmed this. I then mentioned her current life situation and that she is heading on the right pathway, and the spirits are happy with the way she is progressing. I had the word of Dublin enter my mind, she confirmed. I then mentioned an old lady of 5ft tall, roundish build, long grey hair, she confirmed. I said that am seeing a graph like a monitor and someone had passed with a heart condition recently, she confirmed.

1st May 2007

I went to Spiritual Development Class at Whitefield Spiritual Church with my friend Lawrence Simms. All the students were in attendance, and it was my turn to address the class from the Rostrum. I told a short story regarding spirituality. I asked my spirit teachers if I could just have evidence continuously. I directed Peter Clarke if I could work with him, he said yes. I informed him I was being made aware of trouble around his left foot area, he confirmed. I went on to say he had a color and a toy car around him. He said yes. I said bake beans, he smiled and said yes. I said that a spirit shadow had appeared on the wall to the right side of him, and I felt it was a family member. I got the impression this was his spirited father/grandfather, peter confirmed. I then said a male in spirit with one leg could he place him. He said yes. I feel spirit was teaching to deliver knowledge of recent events, which is strong evidence from the spirit world.

20th May 07

It was on this day that it was decided by my spirit energy teachers that I should start to work on their behalf. During my meditation, I understood that a spirit message came to my mind, which stated, 'it is time for you to represent the spirit energy world. It was followed by the name Spirit Teacher, Ronald Baker. I suddenly felt overwhelmed and excited, but I thought to myself I would take it slowly and wait to be asked by the public, spiritual churches, spiritual centers. And for good reasons too.

Later in the afternoon, I observed a young lady near the local town hall wearing what appeared to be a scholar hat, indicating she had finished her university studies. I immediately knew this was a message from the spirit confirming my spirit message.

I understand that I will be continuing to learn about spiritual insights, and I will continue to conduct research and read many spiritual books to broaden the word content in my mind. Even though I have finished my spiritual diary does not mean I have finished my development. I am aware it has just started. The real teaching will begin, learning and gaining experience. I will continue to read books on science, fine arts, music learn about animals and other subjects. I understand that I need to learn how to love and respect all God's creations. Understand what love means and the benefits to my inner spirit for it to grow.

I am my own person and will make my own decisions to help me on my spiritual journey and will not be distracted or dictated to by anyone. However, I am an open-minded person who will listen to any opinions. I understand I am not a special human being, and I will not expect that I will have an advantage in the spirit realm. Like everyone on earth, I must work towards these spiritual goals.

I hope you now have more of an idea of why I suggested that you create your own spiritual dairy from the day you decided to develop your psychic senses. I have mentioned many times to people where all over the world, they have psychic senses that have been dormant for many years. Your sixth sense was at its strongest when you were a child. It was currently you were innocent of the material world we live in. Before you learned how to use your five physical senses, you relied on your sixth sense.

Spiritual work is not only about spirit communication through passing messages but also about how you lead your life on earth. It's the true secret to spiritual growth. My spiritual dairy would have hopefully inspired you or encouraged you to learn about this interesting subject, and like all dairies, they prove to be interesting for the reader and certainly for the author.

I did not write every day about my spiritual experience, the reason why, bust at work, too tired, or there was nothing to write about. That said, there would have been other spiritual experience that I did not enter, but always remember your spirit teachers is always there in the background.

Chapter 15: God is Love (Creator of the Universe)

Plato's statement, "He is the greatest physician who can remove love from where it should not be and place it where it should be," draws attention to the greatest human misdirection of love, the most dynamic force in the universe. When love is misdirected, the very life force is misdirected because God is love. This cause gives rise to the following effects.

- Conjugal love destroys the constancy of affections and causes debauchery when it becomes unsocial, unkind, and bestial.

- Parental love causes spoiled children and, when inverted, a dislike of children.

- Fraternal love causes indiscriminate associations and when inverted hatred, revenge, and wars.

- Filial love causes undue reverence for superiors and, when inverted, disrespect and skepticism.

- Universal love causes hastiness, impetuousness, and unruly power. When inverted, the individual despises him/herself and everybody else and is the greatest power and influence on evil deeds. It is rare that this love becomes inverted, but if it should flow back into the other expressions of love, they will be empowered to

239

accomplish mighty evils under their respective forms of manifestation.

Society advances as man advances and vice versa, but the profit element shows that misdirection self-love demands not `what can we do for each other` but `how may we use each other for personal gain.` However, there are those who see the need to change the basis of commercial life and to produce things for use and not for profit. The harmonical philosophy of spiritualism states that evils we are suffering from arise mainly from the misdirection of self-love, but it will not always be so because the other loves and wisdom attributes slowly awake and clamor for gratification, and misdirected self-love results in the starving of the higher nature. When that goes on for a long time without redress, violent changes take place, and a higher state of civilization is often only reached through a cataclysmic period of destruction - and this is because we will not or cannot open our eyes to our nature and our good.

The doctrine that one member cannot suffer without the other members suffering with it lies at the foundation of social reformation. It is undeniable that the present antagonistic state of the trades and professions generates hurts and animosities among individuals, and it is likewise undeniable that the teachers in all modern theological institutions do very much towards discouraging social and individual reformation by instilling into the present and rising generations the baneful conviction that the world is all a vale of tears under the Adamic curse, suffering the penalty of the original sin: hence, that reformation independent of the church is impossible and is considered impious.

Here we find the influence of certain religious ideas upon our social life. Wrong beliefs, closely-held and instilled into the mind of the child, have a definite influence upon society. The struggle between the various sects to influence the education of the child is evidence of the importance of having true ideals relative to our spiritual nature. To teach men that they are tainted with original sin is to hinder progress, for if it enters consciousness, the individual will not make an effort to rise of him/herself. Indeed, many of the religious conceptions of the western world are wrong and altogether contradictory. On the one hand, the theologians say that man has free will and, on the other, that he is tainted with original sin, i.e., the man has a constitutional bias towards evil. If he has a constitutional bias towards evil, how can he have free will?

The result of this is that man is taught to mistrust his own powers and to look outside for his salvation. There are today thousands of people who are looking to the coming of some great world teacher to pull the world into shape.

241

The world will never be righted in that manner, for a while these people are looking to the coming of some special teacher, they are likely to neglect to try to the right the world themselves.

Chapter 16: Automatic Writing with Spirit Ron Baker

Let me briefly explain Automatic writing. Automatic writing should not be confused with inspirational writing. Automatic writing is where a spirit controls the spirit's medium physical body whilst he/she is in a trance. The medium will not be aware of what has been written, and the writing can be different from the spirit medium's own style of writing.

It has been known that spirits have used both hands of the spirit mediums. This type of spiritual mediumship is a form of a physical phenomenon that is rarely used by spirit mediums of today.

Inspirational writing is when the mental spirit medium relaxes his/her mind and writes down the thoughts that enter their mind. The latter may have the spirit medium's own thoughts added to the script. This type of mediumship is a form of mental phenomenon.

Q.1

Some enlightenment about Reincarnation and Karma would be helpful, please?

A.

Yes, this question has a worldwide appeal and connects with so many schools of thought. Very often where there is no apparent connection. It is very appealing to think that there is a second chance to either get something right or even to improve on previous performance. Moreover, the Laws of the Spirit are the only framework of experience and not man's imaginings. The law is one of moving forward, and one may visualize a vast river of life flowing into the ocean of God. Within that river, various eddies and currents will occur whilst the main body of the river continues flowing in one direction. Thus, it is that reincarnation is not a necessity for every spirit, but those certain circumstances, an irregular flowing within a circle or backward, does take place. This visual model is good to form a background for your thinking in this connection. Remember also that individual lives caught within a given time sequence may bear together the characteristic of the current in which they flow. Thus emerged the concept of group souls and another connection other than time being the spatial concept, may unite spirits which are otherwise quite separate in the time sequence (but ask what time is?). Relate further to this question that the flame of life burns as the Divine Aspect within each one and in this sense every individual life in every other person. Think carefully and deeply on this point. It answers many sub-questions. The body and the ego both belong to form, whilst the spirit belongs to energy consciousness and God. Why then should your idea of the form be so essential to the incarnation of God. It is more truthful to think that Divine Manifestation is refined away from the form dimension and into that of energy for moral and ethical progress: think rather that you have already lived in all previous lives, rather than a selected few. This is nearer the truth than you can imagine and places your thinking into a much higher category in these matters. Also, your life will have been already lived by all those spirits who follow in your earthly pilgrimage. You are then thinking with the mind of God, and this must be better for you in every way.

Q.2

You wrote that I must ask what time it is.

A.

It is well that you ask this now because time is only evident with the experience of your life using 'Form'. When in the outworking of the processes you have done with form and are manifesting as energy in the form of light, time will be meaningless to you. It is only one of those factors produced by the individualized mind. The more you can see it through God's mind, the more whole is the view, and time simply is no more.

Q.3

Can you give some thought to Karma?

A.

Why not when cause and effect, action and reaction, magnetism, and electricity. Acid and alkaline all give evidence to the theme. It is true that as was said of old: There is a time for sowing and a time for reaping. This is Karma, the scales of equipoise, which are struck in every life, the scales are always the instrument of equilibrium, and all things must find their own perfect level. Thus, it remains that Karma shows the law in operation that everything must be earned, especially on spiritual themes. If it is not earned, then it cannot be truly understood or used, so runs God's Perfect Laws.

Q.4

What happens to the body metabolism during the functioning of spirit mediumistic faculties, and what are the sources of energy used physically and psychically during these processes?

A.

The metabolic rates are altered according to the type of spirit mediumship. Thus for mental mediumship, the top three chakras and endocrine glands are involved directly in a quickened state. In physical mediumship, the entire system is directly involved, whilst for trance states, a polarization between the top and the lowest centers is involved. As to sources of energy, they arise mainly from the liver, heart, and pancreas. Coming from heat and friction with glycogen to keep the higher output sustained. A condition of `negative` sensitivity is found throughout the digestive and eliminative processes, and it should be remembered not to fill the stomach after mediumship - until it is positive again after thirty minutes to one hour. Also, consider the adrenals which are triggered, but in a minor way. From energy utilization, the liver is prone to collapse and should be restored with sugar or the same in weak dilution after circles, etc., say two teaspoons in a warm drink. A similar process to the above is found at the etheric level and places the physical body under certain pressure, what you might call psychic energy. Remember also the brain and that increased energy produces more waste, and that the blood can become filled with waste substances temporarily. All energy is God - and illuminates the nervous system in its electrical function. Other energy processes too complex for you to understand may be thought of as reversal or polarizations.

Q.5

To what extent should a medium interpret signs and symbols received for a sitter? Should they be conveyed to a sitter as they are received, or should they be interpreted according to his understanding?

A.

The symbols are the unconscious language of the spirit medium and are unintelligible to the sitter unless they are directly received from the sitter's mind when a different situation is involved. Thus, in the first instance, the spirit medium must interpret, and in the second, the sitter.

Q.6

During the early experiences in meditation, why do some people experience emotional upsets, e.g., floods of tears?

A.

This is due to inner pressures and tensions, which are discharged, just like a circuit between the brain and the nervous system. Call it an `opening` rather than an upset, which it is not. The emotions arise from the etheric level and may be understood as `soul sensing`. Thus in the state, one becomes aware of spiritual reality, also in certain conditions, a feeling which is akin to early protections from the physical body. Thus, it is that those undertaking meditation should be prepared to see themselves at all levels, and from this knowledge of self, a positive personality and attitude to life emerges. In the conditions mentioned, all sensory feelings are temporarily acute or accentuated prior to the state of inner peace, which is the goal a little further on. See the concept of active and passive, positive and negative again is involved. Thus the symptoms of emotional discharge indicate a movement at a much deeper level of the consciousness. For an analogy, consider the minor earthquakes which arise from time to time. Deeper, more central forces break through to the surface with some disruption, but with care and attention, these forces can be harnessed. Also, remember that the symptom does relate to temporary instability and if out of control, is disruptive to good spiritual work. The condition can be helped by vigorous massage of the limbs, solar plexus, and head in that order. This should not be brought out in meditation and not in development classes; otherwise, too much emphasis upon emotional forces produces a negative situation to arise in the developing spiritual medium.

Q.7

There are some frightening accounts of people being scratched and bitten by Poltergeists and of fruit being eaten by invisible entities!

A.

Firstly, consider that man is always afraid of anything which he is unable to understand, and that fear can almost always be traced to a lack of knowledge. When all facts are known and understood, the fear element is replaced by one of natural curiosity and consequent personal growth. The tantrums of a naughty child have no mystery or fear for the experienced nanny, where knowledge and experience indicate the necessary action to take. It is generally felt amongst others and me in spirit that innocent activity is often misinterpreted in your world as a wilful entity when a simple attempt to attract attention may have been the only factor involved. Natural laws are perfect, and every individual is subject to these laws, more so when thoughts of transgression which may harm others are involved. Such wilful spirits are contained entirely within their own `mansion` and are not free to roam the earth world or even into our world. Consider also that specially trained spirits work amongst those of special need in this connection and in order to do their special work must descend (in your terms) to the special mansions or sphere which is involved. Now add to this the fact that psychic energy released unconsciously by people still incarnate may become involved with what you call poltergeist activity, leading to further confusion. Approach the question then, that it is necessary first to separate the different parts which may be involved. Already the mystery and fear begin to fade as the search for knowledge commences.

The question of eating etc. is answered by the fact that only a physical body can digest the food of the earth, and in certain cases, this may be the body of a spirit medium from whom the primary energy was evolved for manifestation. Consider also the apport of food such as may be considered in case of loaves and fishes. When an item is raised above the frequency level of your world, it is invisible; it is invisible to you through fundamentally still part of the etheric sheath, the no sphere of char din. Put another way, the `energy world` from which the `form` world is created constantly recreates the world of forms. From this question, we suggest that you learn to walk without fear but with a natural curiosity to understand all situations and conditions in a manner fitting to a child of God.

Q.8

Please give the forms of mediumship within M.S Capabilities?

A.

There are two factors to consider in this question. First, there is the transmission of a force, power, or quality, quite separate from the information which may be conveyed from one entity to another. This force is the first level of spiritual mediumship which you possess. Remember that the greatest of all gifts is love, and it is this love upon which all other gifts can manifest. Love overcometh all things and is the greatest of all the gifts which will surely pass away, but love alone endures forever. Now, remember that in the form world of which we now speak (having spoken of energy world) that many factors are involved, and that a definite pattern, or better to say a sequence of manifestations, is manifested within the special mediumship qualities which you possess. Hence, we may start with the soul sensing level, what you call psychometry, which for you will open the doorways to many other forms. Think in this manner that by using an `object` to tune in, you are virtually creating a direct line of communication (mediumship) between all intelligence, thought, and memory to which the mind is focused by the attunement process. Follow this level of sensing into the clairvoyant realm, but the psycho or soul sensing will be the more accurate with you. Inner voice speaking is also possible but not so much with outward objective voices, but with inner subjective sounds, for example, the still mind voice.

Spiritual healing comes next, with many sublevels in this area for you to explore. Physical levels are with you also but not to act as the main condenser but to be able to work in assisting someone of greater potential. From what we say, we see that your psychometrical development is given due care and attention in the early days of your development.

Trance (which is on your mind, though at the moment you are trying to block the thought of same), is within your capabilities but in modern form without the necessity for entity control of brain to brain, but with spirit entity controlling at a distance. See this as similar to a long-distance telephone call. The mind all too often is colored or circumscribed by that which has gone before, whereas it is far more important to allow new expressions to formulate and crystallize within the changing march of time, is this not so with music?

Q. 9

Is the mediumship which M.S is using in church functioning at its full capacity?

A.

No, it's not! Remember that it is very rare indeed to function at full capacity. When this may happen within a given moment of time, the spiritual bliss of the mystic is experienced.

Q.10

Can advice be offered in clairvoyance at a spiritual church or center?

A.

Yes, of course, advice can be given. Firstly, lets us take out the word clairvoyance, which supposes that you are seeing all material communicated, which is certainly not the case.

Here in this, our simple advice we can remove an obstacle for you. Think rather that you are going to attempt communication and that the quality and method of this communication will be determined by factors, some of which are beyond your control, for example, the personal worthiness of the recipient, the factors of your own makeup will be adjusted slowly by development. Now then, pay special attention to that which follows, which is of great importance to all spirit mediums who truly wish to improve the quality of their mediumship. It is necessary for the consciousness to function within the four-dimensional context, and to this end, the spirit medium must make a definite effort to sublimate all three-dimensional stimulation and focus. See yourself then rather as a `dead` person trying to communicate with the living recipient. Psychologically this will put you on our side of the fence, where we are better able to impress you. Do not dismiss this simple advice; it is the best. Also, know that the area of the mind which is not native to the three-dimensional or four-dimensional worlds is involved. In other words, you have the ability in your own mind to produce the necessary shift in consciousness, which alone can improve the quality.

Q.11

Does an electrolyte imbalance in the body influence the quality of spiritual mediumship?

A.

No, as already stated, the quality is determined by the shift in consciousness.

Q.12

What factors hinder communication?

A.

All those factors stimulate the sensory pathways.

Q.13

Please enlarge?

A.

The sensory pathways are those physical dimensions roads by which information is conveyed. They only clog up the system higher up in the main lines of communication. A pile-up hinders the free passage of information at higher levels. We say keep the sub roadways clear, and you will have a better transmission at a higher level. It stands to reason surely! The continued passage of spiritual information helps in the maintenance of these higher routes. But the explanation is pure logic.

Q.14

Please explain polarization.

A.

Yes. View this as an explosive separation of the Divine Mother and Divine Father in order that the connection (Child of God) may be understood. Thus, anything which separates represents a separation in the Divine Polarity which is necessary for all new forms to come into being, also for the regeneration of old forms. (This could open a medical aspect).

Q.15

Please explain `the regeneration of old forms!

A.

Yes, it's our pleasure, at last, you are getting nearer to the center of the question. `Old Forms` means that wherever form exists, the separated polarity upon which its existence depends is naturally becoming drawn together in the marriage of the divine Father and Mother, which would cause the form to vanish away. However, the `Old form` is regenerated by holding the electro-magnetic polarity in a stable condition so that the electro-magnetic is the only polarity that bridges into the four-dimensional world and beyond.

Q.16

Information on sender, please?

A.

To you, I am the archetypal form of academic and scholar. I am the composite of all such who have entered the form world from the world devoid of form.

Q.17

What are you to yourself?

A.

I am the distillation of all thought and experience, only having personality and identity within the Divine Father and Divine Mother. My polarity long since ceased, and my form vanished away, but I can live and transmit by using your forms.

Q.18

Is the link between yourself and the spirit medium direct?

A.

Yes, more direct than you can imagine, but it is between the two of you that an electro-magnetic arc has occurred, thus producing the radiance in which I now stand (Metaphorically).

Q.19

Is Spirit Communication with X.X or Y.Y. possible?

A.

Spirit Communication should never be forced in any way, and it is not a good time to communicate at the moment due to the fact that the higher areas of the spirit medium's brain have been illumined by the great minds which have been in contact, making it more difficult for ordinary communication to take place. Rather like asking for musical scales from one who has just played an intricate passage of music. However, in the case of the lady, we are aware that some residual experience of unconsciousness is still evident in her present position, and it remains unlikely for the present that communication would take place.

Q.20

Explain Please?

A.

Self-explanatory. Note that we state some residual experience, for example, the memory of the previous condition, and this entity has had other conditions to follow - not too much in the way of spirit intercourse here.

Q.21

Explain Please?

A.

Yes, into those areas of life experience denied, the entity now moves forward in exploring those polarities in form manifestation vital to the soul mission.

Q.22

What is the purpose of being homosexual?

A.

The purpose here is not a good word. It does not convey the question properly because homosexuality is the window through which the world is viewed. We might as well say, what is the purpose of wearing spectacles? Thus, homosexuality is a condition that assists the entity to better achieve its soul's mission.

Q.23

What is the precise cause of homosexuality?

A.

The same as the cause of heterosexuality.

Q.24

Why does society condemn homosexuality?

A.

Only parts of society do this in your geographical location. Consider in other sections of society a different approach. However, the reason is that society always tries to overthrow that which does not conform whether right or wrong does not enter the argument.

Q.25

Why are there such wide differences in life experience, bearing in mind that

Reincarnation seems to be the exception rather than the rule.

A.

Why only one flower, one tree, one butterfly, etc.? The expression of Divine Life is one of unending variety and manifestation. The computations are like the cells in the body. This last sentence has two meanings, one much deeper than the words appear to convey.

Q.26

Please explain the latter half of the question?

A.

Good! You are learning to focus your questions. The cell is a balanced energy form between positive and negative, active and passive, alkaline and acid, etc. It polarizes (In the world of energy, the requirement is not the same.) So, the homosexual may be seen to expand also within the world of form in order to gain vital and necessary information which will enter later stages of soul development. Only in the world of form do the oppositions occur with such separated functions. In the energy world, there is a total expression.

Q.27

Please give the precise cause of backache in the cervical region.

A.

Yes, slight displacement in the lumbar region. The third lumbar needs to be eased. This imbalance throws the higher position out rather, like harmonic relationships known in engineering by another name.

Q.28

Please advise on treatment.

A.

Yes, direct the spiritual healing forces from your own mind into the target area of your third lumber; this follows ipso facto. Lie face down on the floor; bring right leg up sideways, bending at the knee until a position of natural tension is reached. Then a helper should lift the left shoulder gently whilst concentrating upon the Lumbar area. This will suffice at present.

Q.29

Please describe the long-term effects on the physical and other bodies of narcotic drugs, which create a sense of unreality or `escapes` in the individual?

A.

These are too varied to generalize, but the basic effect is to cause a breakdown of orderly communication between the brain of the physical and etheric bodies. Just as the interplay exists between the inner and outer brains so, this reflects as the signals are `stepped` up for a reception at the etheric level. Anesthetics have a similar effect. Now realize that the brain is the coordination center of the whole organism. Consequently, the eccentric, nervous electrical activity is reflected in a degenerative way throughout the whole. The `escape` mentioned is more properly described as a momentary collapse of the communications system, like pulling out the plug. Now give the following full consideration in your thinking. The long-term effect is to deny real experience to the victims. Consequently, he/she is robbed of the most precious gift of all. However, properly controlled for pain relief, etc. It is elevated to the `mercy` level and becomes positive in its effect.

The breakdown of communication (cerebral) is reflected by a spastic condition in certain cells, which, through becoming charged in a negative force, are slowly paralyzed or prevented from sustaining the health of the whole. Consider also that the effects are often, if not always, observed firstly in the cells, before in the behavior of the entity. As above also below. Study the body from biological and microscopic levels, also the emotional and spiritual effects at the energy level. The future will bring the application of micro-electrical stimulation for medical needs, rather than the `heavier` drug forms now in use, and botanic drugs will become outmoded.

Q.30

Where does the soul originate from, and before it takes its earthly form, is it an Individual entity or part of a greater consciousness?

A.

Let us qualify the word soul as the personal consciousness, issuing forth from a central source and possessing all the elements of same. Thus, it has always contained the principle of the whole and the principle of individualization. Know also that it vibrates within a harmonic scale, groups with other entities of the same, `note` or vibration which is determined by the soul mission. Further to this, know that entities within a group are equal and no hierarchical system is involved. However, when the experience of each entity has expanded the inner consciousness, group consciousness is perfected and maybe the last process before returning to the Central Source.

Q.31

If reincarnation is the exception rather than the rule, why is there such a variation in the life experience and situations on earth?

A.

The variations are greater when viewed from the realm of form, whereas when considered as the pulsation of energy, a clearer image is obtained as in the manifestation of a single rainbow. Remember that the single unit of light is part of the whole manifestation, though it reflects a special quality (color) according to the soul mission.

Let each then be according to his lights.

Q.32

Who or what forces decide which earthly circumstances or life pattern the soul is drawn towards on the earth plane?

A.

The Divine Parents through those laws and principles governing same and with certain independent controls operated by the entity within the given impulse guiding the manifestation of same.

Q.33

If it is possible for entities of higher intelligence to communicate with us and to influence us in certain aspects of our lives, surely it is logical to assume that it is possible for entities of low intelligence and with perhaps malicious intent to influence us also?

A.

Perhaps if we replace the word intelligence with Godliness, it becomes clearer for you to understand. The more `Godly` are entitled to use energy etc., in the process of communications, whereas the less Godly or the `ungodly` are not. This is the simple fact power is not placed in the hands of ignorant entities, and it is only attained by those who, by their own spiritual evolution, has merited its use.

Q.34

We often hear from spirit mediums that a child is growing up in the spirit. Why can the child not revert to its existence prior to earthly incarnation?

A.

But this is exactly what happens. The entity reverts to the previous sphere of that prior to physical incarnation. Remember, the life journey of souls is inconceivable in terms of duration or time in your dimension. Viewed as an Eternal Journey, the physical step which appears so important to you is viewed by us as being in tandem with early etheric spheres.

Q.35

What is the precise role of spirit helpers during mediumship?

A.

To cooperate in the expression of spiritual truth and manifestations, arising from the incarnation of the two worlds.

Q.36

Please give a detailed description of the mechanics of spiritual mediumship from the point of view of the communicator as well as the medium.

A.

The radiant energy of the communicator is used to produce telepathic waveforms, which span the distance between the communicator and the medium. From this, realize that it is not necessary for the spirit communicator to be near the medium but may choose to influence from a distance. Thus, one is the transmitter, and the other is a receiver with telepathic waveforms connecting one to the other. From the communication view, energy is used and directed outward, whilst from the medium's viewpoint. Energy is received or registered as an external impingement upon the consciousness. Know also that the signals are amplified as they pass from the receptors in the etheric body down via the natural route to the physical brain and conscious mind. It is then the etheric brain and subconscious mind first, then the physical brain and conscious mind second. In those forms of communication which involve physical energy, the first step is similar, but great pressure is manifested throughout the nervous system of the medium in order to release bioplasmic energy, call it ectoplasm. The same applies in trance conditions where the radiant energy, being of a more powerful nature, prevents the normal electro-nervous impulses from registering in the cerebral cortex. Various novel conditions do exist in particular forms of mediumship, but it would be necessary to explore these as individual projects.

Q.37

During, for example, a private setting, does all the information received by the spirit medium come from spirit helpers or the recipient's relatives? If not, what are the other sources of information?

A.

Remember that a medium is an interpreter of information received and consequently may produce alterations, interpolation, and omissions according to conditions prevailing at the time. However, any mind which is connected or for whatever reason may subscribe to the communication. Also, the deep consciousness of the medium may search for supplementary information, from the mind of the communicator or from any other source which is open to it. View it as a collective effort, often bearing the overall personality of a particular individual.

Q.38

Must all "Cause and Effect" be equalized in the earthly experience, or is it carried over to the next existence?

A.

Effects from earthly causes are carried forward into the spirit world, at the point of transition.

Q.39

It has been said that certain types of music have healing properties. Can this theory be explained, please?

A.

Yes, the sound is fundamental to the creation of form and to its ongoing existence. "In the beginning was the word and word were with God" Also, the vibrational emphasis of AUM is known to produce certain elevated or spiritual effects. Now consider that a cosmic "chord" holds all universal energy and form together, rather like beads threaded upon a "chain of sound". Within the atom exists the sound of its own formation and activity even as the same is reflected upon the harmonic scale upwards to the Milky Way Galaxy? Then upward again to harmonize with other galaxies. Perhaps already you will see that sound, whether harmonious or discordant, reflects forwards and backward as circular ripples upon a vibrating universe. Such a scale may be seen to exist within the physical body. Then on a higher scale, the etheric body and even higher to encompass the spirit. Healing music is harmonizes the different levels of man's self.

Drawing in, the different incorporated sounds into a harmonious direction. For an analogy, consider the iron filings aligning themselves in response to the applied magnetic field. Therefore sound, properly applied, brings the denser components into a state of harmony within the field which contains them. Know also that just as each entity vibrates in a particular manner, so also musical compositions are endless in character and quality. For experimentation and the best therapeutic results, it is necessary to exclude other sensory material, and it will be found advantageous to use the light in the indigo or deep purple register to complement music therapy. However, much work will need to be done before establishing the best methods and conditions, etc. Observations of bodily cycles, sounds, rhythms, etc., may give some insight into music which would harmonize at a physical level refine upward to etheric level. Sound is part of the great energy spectrum, and it must be remembered that it is one of many important keys while color is another important key. Research can also start by analysis of musical likes and dislikes of different personality types. Volume levels also are important, depending greatly upon how the sound is used either to enhance life experience or to `drown` it out; each aspect has something to teach.

Q.40

Much has been spoken of the so-called `Golden Age`, which is to come. What major changes will take place in the world in order that this be achieved?

A.

The greatest change is to be within mankind in the development of the spiritual (Golden) qualities which will lay the foundations for the building of the Kingdom. The Summerland upon Earth. Before this phase, there will be many geographical changes as Mother Nature prepares for the coming epoch. A man may attune himself, however, to the coming changes and thereby cooperate in the changing scene rather than become the victim of it, as so many fears. The greatest lesson which confronts mankind at present is the formation of World Brotherhood and Sisterhood. To this add a changing economic structure, away from wasteful overproduction, towards production for use combining that which endures and lasts rather than that which perishes too soon also a greater emphasis upon food as medicine, and

271

preventative steps in what are now considered major health risks.

Q.41

Can we receive any diagnostic guidance for M.S?

A.

It is always possible to receive guidance on the matter of health, the problem being that such advice is not acceptable to those having control over such matters of health culture in your space-time quantum. However, the subject is underscan, and the information is as follows. One of the main areas of imbalance is within the moisture and dryness of the physical organism. Thus, all components which have an effect upon the moisture or dryness of any part of this body are of importance, consider particular the implications from the actual biological and physiological dimensions and then into microscopic levels. Thus, salt, which is the trigger in many of these levels, may be taken in the homeopathic preparation to bring back a better-organized equilibrium throughout the whole. Remember also that the electrical energies and flows which regulate the actual expansion of life elements are dependent at the physical level upon the correct interplay between the dry and moist surfaces. Guard against these areas which naturally fall within this principle. Pleurisy and all inflammations of the mucous membranes where an excess of fluid may cause the setting up of toxins which are transmitted then into other parts to do their damage when the original site of their manufacture has long since been forgotten. View each part and symptoms separately in the light of what is given weigh carefully in the scales of your own knowledge with every modern consideration when the greatest benefits from this knowledge may be yours. Yes, the skin turns dry and wet, and truth may be seen. Also, in the saliva, when excesses have manifested followed by an abnormal drying, a symptom of diabetes which one can discount for you as the process involved in the sugar condition is not directly involved here, but only in animated form pseudo not real. This will be well received! Now on to more direct information. The blood conditions have been under discussion. The basic elements are in saline or salt in the blood giving greater precipitation factor to the insulin unknown by you doctors as such. Thus the magnetic flux of the blood is affected and, in turn, affects those elements which ride through it. Again, correct this by using that already given, and the factors may be produced in this body which will tend to normalize and allow the sugar metabolism, which is one and an octave farther on than salt, to be correctly and electrically discharged through the blood stream and permit of no further repercussion in the kidneys and bladder these have been caused by too great a pressure

273

which is built up by excessive salinity in the blood. The body is important to you now, but what of the mind, which is of greater importance in these times past and in times present and to come. The subject is an illumined one, not saint, not a flaming or exalted one, but one who has been kindled into flame and now waits to light up the area of experience to which he has been sent.

All things are revealed by light, never by darkness, ignorance, or bigotry. Take a torch, and with the mind no longer afraid, go forward on a pathway illumined from the inner perceptiveness of your own being. He who has the power to think also has the power to be used in the transmission of thought, such as which this is an example of. Yeah, it is to be said here that he is a terminal point, a delicately tuned receiving instrument that will be used for uses of filling out the power of good in the world. Thus, a bridge of communications is made between him and us, which he may use. (Question asked mentally regarding the type of mediumistic ability the subject possesses). Yes, your question, but always remember that the extent to which we may impress is without a doubt limited by factors present in your personality and by your experiences and practice. Why waste time? We say to you again we have extended the bridge now, and only a fool climbs down the hill to cross when a new bridge lies straight ahead. Do not be afraid but use the bridge. Walk across it many times until you really believe that it is yours. Through familiarity, you make it yours. Dare we say you understand this? You ask how! But have we not shown you how in this example? No problem, no fuss, no bother, just writing a letter. Ask the question, receive the answer. Nothing could be easier. Yes, yes, now you know your impulse to buy a paper before mentioned to the instrument earlier before the dusk had gathered the corners of your world for the night. Guided, guided, guided, told, told, told, but still, you wait. Wake up and recognize that you must play your part. Nothing happens in isolation. If our instrument had not taken up the pen, you could not have this but believe us when we say it has all been very carefully arranged so that this important fact could be brought home to you. Now go, we must too much distortion - like short circuits in the brain of an instrument. Go in peace and love.

Q.42

Who or what force is responsible for controlling the power mentioned in the question on communication? (Q.33)

A.

The Divine Mind or understood the better, as that emerging spark of divinity within the individual.

Q.43

Please expand on `Laws and Principles` and certain independent controls` as mentioned in the answer beginning, `The Divine Parents through those laws, etc.? (Q.32)

A.

The laws and principles are those fixed attributes of Divine Mind, which you may think of as the very important framework or web of creation, over which the tapestry of life is spread out. Another way is to see those terms as expressing the character of God. Certain independent controls refer to the exercise of will by the entity but remember that this itself is limited by the circumstances surrounding the same environment, soul mission, etc.

Q.44

Please give the causes of carcinoma with reference to medical terminology and to question of `regeneration` of old forms and electromagnetic polarity? (Q.14 & 15)

A.

To provide the information requested, it is not possible to refer throughout to medical terminology, which would only restrict the information. To obtain the best results, let us be free to communicate these thoughts and concepts, which will be the most productive of new lines of inquiry to you. At the evolutionary level, some forms may seem to belong to a `fungoid` fungus stage of development as parasitic cells grow in a free situation, say on the surface of a tree. The reflections downwards into different layers of the physical body may also be found to reflect into certain evolutionary development through which the body has passed, blood cancer, relating to the sea, and bone cancer, more to the mineral processes of evolution. In this area alone, there is much which is said once the right minds are brought into conjunction together. Here the question of regeneration of old forms may be understood as the healing process meaning directly that `old forms` example, the matter which is locked in or connected to some evolutionary development of past, must be freed by the regeneration of energy to prevent these throwbacks from manifesting. The key lies within the endocrine system and its electromagnetic balance, importunely unknown yet to your medical researchers. The harmony and balance of the whole organism largely depend upon the good working of the endocrine system, which, in turn, through its ability to accelerate or decrease certain functions and processes, must be recognized as a vital element in connection with this question. In the stresses of life combined with other factors, the endocrine system is under constant pressure, more so when it is appreciated that every thought and feeling, every emotion, has a direct effect upon the endocrine tree. Also,

277

take heed of cell growth in the first weeks of pregnancy and the processes involved therein, also the special evolutionary contingencies which can and do arise from time to time. Further, consider the process involved in prenatal endocrinology and the need to ensure harmonious development throughout. All too often, in present-day conditions, the endocrine pressure goes unnoticed, but the negative effects of the same accumulate through hundreds of years, even into third and fourth generations. Know also that interference with hormonal balances in child prevention etc., produces the same negative vibrations to arise. Seek rather to work within the balanced framework of the central source than to impose alterations upon the same, which are in contradiction to the purpose involved. Cell growth in cancer is a contradiction of the ordered, planned, harmonious, and light bringing forces associated with all spiritual manifestations. Now, the relationship in electromagnetic polarity with direct bearing is one of stimulation and activity, against dormancy and passivity is the proper balance between the opposing energies within the organism, not only at the personal thinking level but also how such thinking and feeling affects the cells. Sufficient for the present time.

Q.45

What factors determine the primary site of a carcinoma?

A.

Those factors at the cell level permit agitation of the electromagnetic field, causing the first depletion of electric energy, followed by too much electrical energy reflected in the magnetic fields. Problems in controlling relate to blood circulation and the nervous system, both of which sustain conditions of the primary site.

Q.46

Please give advice on the best form of spiritual healing to give relief from the suffering of a terminal illness.

A.

Knowledge of the situation of the patient for the full cooperation of the life force with the transition process instigated by same. In some cases, the moral support and personal warmth of the healer will work wonders, but it is not possible to generalize for every Person is different. The best healing must be that which is entered into with conscious knowledge of both.

Q.47

If euthanasia were to become common practice, would this not deprive the personal consciousness of vital experience in the life pattern? Experience which is available perhaps only in the earthly existence?

A.

When a full stop is reached in any manifestation, a conversation takes place, opening the next phase. This is the Law. Remember that man can work within the law as his power and ability to use the same increase. Here there is no robbery, only the hand which reaches out to help.

Q.48

Please give the processes, Laws, and materials involved in the production of materialization?

A.

The Laws of mediumship combined with a movement of plasma from the medium's physical body and through the same. This, together with corresponding plasma from the spirits involved, makes the polarity activate for the pseudo manifestation of form.

Q.49

Please explain the mechanics of Automatic Writing.

A.

In our own case, a simple mental control is exercised, which directs those unconscious levels of the mind normally involved in writing.

Q.50

Please describe the sphere of existence passed through by the soul on its eternal journey.

A.

Too vast to describe in detail but best thought of as passing from the formed into the formless from darkness into light. A transition to a higher vibration of life.

Q.51

What is the cause of ulcerative colitis, and, with reference to medical terminology, what is the best treatment for this disease?

A.

The cause is often found to be linked with poor ability to digest animal foods, particularly the by-products of dairy classification. The rejection of the body associated with repelling of obnoxious substances introduced into the same may be seen as the cause of primary irritation and early inflammation to the digestive processes. Soon the secretion of the stomach, gall bladder, liver, pancreas, and spleen are all subject to acid imbalance, and the electrical quality of the intestine is weakened. The condition is probably aggravated by the ingestion of antibiotics etc., by the animals, the altered chemicals of which are taken into the body. Thus, it should be profitable to remove all links between patient and animal world and seek to antidote any drug residues received in the same manner, especially where dairy products are known to aggravate the situation. Mild electrical stimulations along the lower two thoracic, lumbar, and sacral spine are also helpful in assisting the electrical balance of the intestine. Fruits and leafy vegetables, whole bread, water, sundries, fruit, oats, and bran may provide the best diet. Generally, note that the body is under an invasion of irritants and toxins, which must be removed if harmony is to be restored. At the present stage of knowledge, homeopathic forces will serve best in directing bodily energies for health, electromagnetic balance, and harmony. Keep the lymph systems working well, and all eliminative processes - especially bowels and kidneys some alteration may also be found in cerebrospinal fluid.

Q.52

Please explain energy.

A.

The energy that is withdrawn from the biological organism, for example, from cells composing the same of whatever plane of vibrations or manifestation.

Q.53

In what ways do "effects" from earthly "causes" influence us after the transition?

A.

In every way, remembering that every thought is a `blueprint` from which the future is unfolded. No lesson may be ignored, and every experience has its essence of the future, which may be understood as moving towards or away from the Divine Light.

Q.54

Please explain the "Central Source" as mentioned in the question, "Where does the soul originate from?" (See Q.30)

A.

The gateway of light, the two pillars which are the Divine father and mother, between which the vortex of creation is manifested. Poetry expresses a concept of measureless proportion.

Q.55

Does the group consciousness mention in the same answer (Q.30) function on all levels of existence or only in the spirit world?

A.

On all levels, the group consciousness manifests and may be seen partly in the natural process of grouping in your earth world. It can also be seen in affinities that transcend casual contact.

Q.56

How are the individual vibration rate and soul mission of an entity determined?

A.

By the inherent "tuning" of the divine spark from its beginning as an individualized entity containing remember, the Divine thought of its moment of separation from the whole. Thus, it is at the precise moment that the previous experienced of all returning entities are breathed into the new pilgrim. Thus, the information from experience sweeps like a tidal wave to and fro in the cosmos.

Q.57

What is the purpose of the chakra system in the body, and how does it function?

A.

The Chakra system is in the etheric body, motivating the endocrine glands of the physical body. It is the electromagnetic system parallel to the acid-alkaline system of your physical body. It serves to enable the life force to feed the body and allow you to walk upon the `ocean bed` of your earth world without drowning. It functions through the basic laws of electromagnetism, attraction, and repulsion. As the God-man attraction is truly activated, the energy system is transformed into a great light from the formed to formless from darkness to light.

Q.58

What are the functions of the chakras in the body, and what is the relationship to spiritual healing?

A.

The function of the major chakras is to form the electromagnetic connections, which are vital to the endocrine glands of the physical body. The body cannot function without these connections. In spiritual healing, they can be used to convey the life force light, these energizing cells which may respond to this stimulation.

Q.59

Please explain how spiritual healing is achieved.

A.

The methods are numerous as man's ingenuity remembers that your medical or scientific methods are only aspects of spiritual healing, for all healing comes from the spirit. Fundamental healing works when organized cells are helped towards proper electrical and chemical functions.

Q.60

Do changes in body chemistry occur when two people fall in love?

A.

Fall in love, fall in light, fall in God. Yes, love makes the necessary electrical connection permitting manifestation of the Divine Light at all levels. At the physical level, the effects are visible in the body via the luminosity of the skin, the magnetic force of the eyes, the improved buoyancy of the whole organism, etc. The increased light energy causes a super-efficient interplay of chemical processes. To experience love is to touch the Divine Light; the next step is to reflect the light outwards. See like pins on a magnet; the force is passed to another.

Q.61

How does a Soul Entity become attached to a particular fetus at conception?

A.

Through the electromagnetic waves emitted by the fertilized cell thus, the individualized spirit commences its vibration descent into the world of form.

Q.62

Are some souls born into physically or mentally handicapped bodies knowingly as part of their life pattern or experience, or is this purely accidental?

A.

It is not the conscious choice of the entity, neither can it be said to be the result of pure accident. Remember that all entities live in the one and one in others, individualization makes this difficult for you to understand, but you must realize that the divine spark within is in constant communication with the central source from which it has been sent forth and to which it must return. It is not the responsibility of the one entity to take on special restrictions in the world of form, but for all other entities to overcome such problems through increasing the knowledge of the same in order to avoid the circumscription of their brother. Such situations reveal the growing, evolving, and perfecting aspects of the central source rather than choice by the incarnating entity. Thus, it is that out of chaos, the order is called forth by the sound of manifestation. Now, remember that nothing is accidental but that the harmonics of the group Soul produce effects, often misinterpreted as previous experience in another form. (See A. & A71)

Q.63

If a child's life was prematurely ended and his intentions had been experiencing an earthly existence. Surely at some future point in time will still have to gain earthly experience.

A.

Earthly experience is important to you because you are in its plane of experience. It is, however, continuous into the first spiritual dimension, and you will come to understand that death is only a footbridge between two planes, which are amazingly similar. Instead of 'earthly experience,' substitute `first plane experience,` and the need for earthly experience will be understood as not being vital. Earthly experience is now much enhanced than earlier stages in man's evolution, but imperfections continue to cause premature transitions. All entities gather experience for the whole and not for the self. Thus an entity may be carried forward for reasons. If the purpose was for self alone, it might be argued differently, but such is not the case.

Q.64

Are spirit entities allowed to communicate with whoever they please, or are there any limitations placed upon them?

A.

They are subject to laws governing the same, which are mainly determined by the Divine light. The more God-like the entity, the greater is the privilege of communication. The ability to communicate is proportionately decreased in those whose light transmission is poor.

Q.65

How does earthly cause and effect influence us in the next existence?

A.

This polarity produces its own reconciliation quality as opposing forces are weighed and equalized.

Q.66

What form did the life pattern of M.S. take in existence previously to this one?

A.

Your life pattern is instilled at the point of individualization from the Central Source. It does not change. However, you are linked to other entities through the group soul harmonics, one such having been a Royal Prince of Persia versed in astrological knowledge, having been tutored by Indian and Arabian Scholars and vibrating harmonically with a Tibetan Monk. In the ancient power of mind and spirit, with a special interest in the qualities of sound, music, pageant, and ritual. The many within the Group Soul these are, but two, who through their experience has prepared the path for you, and whose minds produce harmonic chords within your consciousness. Thus, it will be until the greater and lesser chords vibrate in perfect unison and from the group a pure tone emerges.

Q.67

Is the transformation in consciousness immediate at the time of transition, or does it take some time for the entity to adjust to the new surroundings and new form of existence?

A.

Usually, the adjustment is gradual, dependent upon the spiritual awareness of the entity.

Q.68

Is it possible for entities now in the earthly existence to have been associated in the level of experience prior to this one?

A.

Yes, with reference to the group soul consciousness and its contribution to the entity like unplumbed currents within the ocean depths.

Q.69

Please give guidelines for achieving the necessary shift in consciousness to improve the quality of mediumship.

A.

Spiritual awareness, divine love, and light permeate at all levels of consciousness. Thus, it was given to seek first the 'inner Kingdom, to which all other things would be added. Think so of consciousness coming from within and not the normal process of the external senses. In this way, the shift in consciousness is achieved, and communication arises from within analogous to a crystal spring bubbling from hidden depths.

Q.70

Please enlarge on "the areas of the mind not native to third or fourth dimensional Worlds?" (A.10)

A.

The advanced function of the mind can only be unfolded when its polarities and dualistic expressions have been resolved. Then, instead of partial utilization, the mind functions are expressed in a total manner. It is this higher Mind function that is not native to the early periods of experience both in earthly and spiritual dimensions. It is simply a matter of the advanced mental function when the mind is used in the fullest sense.

Q.71

Please expand on the statement, "Every individual life in every person? (A.1 & A.62).

A.

Simply the fact that every life is a manifestation of God, and the Divine Spark resides equally in every individualised entity. Thus, God lives in all, and each entity must in every other soul exist.

Q.72

Please give an account of what happens in the next dimension to one who commits suicide?

A.

It depends upon the casual factors and motive, amongst other things. However, as a general guide, they have shown great understanding of the compassion by those whose mission is to help as guides. This is a temporary breakdown in the soul's mission and is healed by love. Loved ones gather to the soul in need and bless with their love the new arrival. The Angels of Light, Spiritual Guardians, then administer with the good counsel to the individual's `need, and the way ahead is planned. Only when the motive is to deliberately cause hurt or pain to another is the entity contained within the limitations imposed, as protection, until the mind is healed.

Q.73

When there are numerous depressed or disturbed or distressed people present during a demonstration of mediumship, it is possible that the mediumship could be adversely affected, and if so, how can the medium protect him/her or "shut out" these disturbing thought forces?

A.

Any vibration of discord will cause adverse situations to arise. Only by the development of God's consciousness can the condition be overcome darkness gives way to light. However, it is sometimes impossible to overcome the negative vibration, and such situations should be recognised and avoided. It all depends upon the strength of God's Consciousness of the individual at a given time and place. When the inner light is weak, it is best to avoid opening spiritually, mediumistic mentally, or psychically. Learn to recognise the situation and cast not pearl before swine.

Q.74

What sexual experience is available in the next dimension?

A.

Same as your present dimension, but with added refinements and developments. The spirit is sexless and functions temporarily through a sexually polarised body. At your physical level, there is an exchange of energy when sexual experience is the expression of love. Eventually, the radiation of spiritual energy, from one to the other, is complete without body contact in a sexual sense. This is most difficult for you to understand but consider that orgasm is for the receiving as well as the expanding of energy. Only when connected at all levels, can a full interchange of energy take place? Thus, the language of love is demonstrated by a flow of energy as life flows out to life, and the God within is joined to the Divine spark of the beloved.

Q.75

Is spirit communication with M.S. possible, and if so, a description of her new life and work would be welcomed?

A.

No longer hindered and circumscribed by earth conditions but free in movement and in mind. She reaches out to the compassionate level of spiritual manifestation as a Spiritual Mother to Souls passing in loneliness and feeling alone. She surrounds the same with a feeling of being wanted, being loved, being important to God, each in their own way. She has needed much time to rise above the conditions of her earthly life, which imprisoned the splendour which was the true nature of her spirit.

Q.76

How is the molecular structure of material altered in order to raise it above the frequency level of this world?

A.

Firstly, a container or vacuum is created as a womb to receive the item. Within this, light is built to invade the atoms involved. Light comes via the mind and thinking the object into a higher frequency. The light accelerates according to the thought. This power is "idioplasmic," under the influence of the mind.

Q.77

How is psychic surgery achieved?

A.

In numerous ways, but usually with a directing intelligence from our world who can manipulate energy in the same way that a surgeon uses a scalpel.

Q.78

Would it be true to say that those spiritually unevolved entities may never succeed, or even at-tempt communication with us? (Q 33)

A.

When they have experienced remorse, the light transmission is increased, with consequent possibilities of communication afforded to them. An only genuine desire for light can rise such a spirit and place them in the Divine Light.

Q. 79

Please give further information on vibration descent.

A.

Yes, the individual passes from the Central Source to the Group Soul and is clothed with the group experience, slightly slowing the emanation vibration to that of the Central Source. The entity passes through many phases (In my Father's House), and each slows the emanation until the entity is ready for the coarsest form of all that of earth.

Q. 80

Can people who direct malicious thoughts towards others cause them actual harm?

A.

It can cause a feeling of ill-ease, but no harm actual harm can result directly at a physical level.

Q. 81

Please give a further discourse on the etheric body.

A.

It is to us in spirit what the physical body is to you on earth. It is truly an energy body the same as the physical, only made from a more highly refined substance, vibrating at a higher frequency. It, too, must die and be shed in the process of moving forward.

Q. 82

Please comment further on reincarnation.

A.

We have commented enough for the present time but let us add further that the entity which rests in the Group Soul carries many of the impressions and experiences of that group, an incident which is often wrongly thought of as indicating reincarnation.

Q. 83

Please expand on answer 35.

A.

Simply to advise as a good teacher, with those methods and techniques which will prove helpful in carrying out Soul Mission. Too much personal feeling is focused, whereas a sense of detachment gives the best results.

Q. 84

How is an entity affected by the termination of pregnancy?

A.

The entity is shocked. So it is that such an entity is in a condition very similar to catalepsy and remains so until, through the compassion and love of those helpers surrounding the entity, is assured that he/she will not be attacked again.

Q. 85

What effects to the terminator exist?

A.

The forgiveness of the entity in the spirit world must be obtained, as they alone can absolve the person or persons involved. However, this is altered according to the motives of the terminator. Very often, they act from ignorance in the name of accepted scientific practice, but how does this give back the experience which has been removed?

Q. 86

Can the entity take another female's body?

A.

No! The magnetic and electrical connections are for that mother and cannot be made over to someone else.

Q. 87

How does the entity progress without the earthly experience?

A.

By proxy with other entities within the group souls. Also, remember that the one lives in all and that all live in the one.

Q. 88

What factors decide the type of mediumship one possesses?

A.

The connections between the two bodies the ability to consciously activate the etheric senses are of prime importance. The mental stability of an individual and the psychological strength of them. The ability to love and not let love become inverted into hatred and jealousy is also not only involved but evident at your level.

Q. 89

Does mediumship adversely affect the pancreas?

A

The effect is not direct, but through the tissues composing the body and with reference to moisture-bearing tissues and the build-up of fats within the body. Thus, it is that does whose metabolism tends to the mediumistic are described as `sensitive` Note that diabetics generally are also "sensitive" people, and the link becomes obvious. It is the intensity of mental energy which is passed back through the nervous system where the trouble lies, though in this case, the kidneys become the buffer with abnormal workings of the adrenal glands in those of sensitive and mediumistic temperament. This is more evident in trance and physical mediums. Sleep is the opposite of stimulation.

Q. 90

Some comments would be appreciated on the mental illness and probable methods of treatment in the future.

A.

Very often, the electrical connections between the hypothalamus and the cortex are out of phase with a condition also existing in the brain stem which interferes adversely with the coordination of the two brains (we mean the etheric and physical brains and not the two parts of the brain). Also greatly affected by chemical disturbances, particularly within the brain fluid itself, much work in the future will depend upon the examination of cerebral fluids and adjustment of the same through chemotherapy. Electrical stimulation (refined), not E.C.T. under any circumstances, may give rich dividends. Also, consider the subconscious mind as a repository for all forces of the past in man's mental and psychological evolution. It is necessary to realise that many cannot cope with the structure of civilisation and would benefit greatly from living simple lives close to the earth in every way. The aggressive temperament particularly would benefit from living cloistered lives, obtaining their own food, clothing, shelter, etc.; the list is endless.

Q. 91

Do all people mix freely after transition, or do they congregate according to colour, race?

A.

Freedom is a condition of spiritual awareness. Thus those of a spiritually awakened condition can enjoy complete freedom of movement. Others are held by those barriers of wrong thinking which divide mankind and which must be overcome in the early stages of spirit life. Also, know that there is no difference between spiritually aware individuals, regardless of ethnic or religious matters.

Q. 92

Is there a stage or plane to which we will eventually progress where communication with the earth plane is no longer possible?

A.

Not so much impossible, but no longer desired, answers this question. Consider also a point that will be reached eventually when the earth's planet will be no more.

Q. 93

Is any benefit gained by becoming vegetarian?

A.

Yes, providing that the diet is adequate to the needs of the body. We foresee a time when meat-eating will be no more, and the evolutionary processes in the human family will become more positively 'tuned' and harmonious in manifestation.

Q. 94

Does sexual polarity still exist in the next dimension, and if so, is it possible to produce children?

A.

The sexual polarity continues in accordance with the advancement of the individual but will eventually be resolved away as finer forms are adopted. Know that only the body of a child is produced by the parent and not the actual child. Something similar but not the same can occur in our world, and it is dependent upon an entity that has been deprived of an earthly body.

Q. 95

Do all illnesses and diseases cease to exist after the transition?

A.

Yes, although some may carry the memory of same for some time like a bad habit.

Q. 96

When spirit entities return to work through a medium, why do they sometimes manifest with the physical conditions which they possessed before their transition?

A.

Some do this for recognition by loved ones and friends. Also, when contacting earth vibrations, memories of the earth are often produced at what you know as the subconscious level of the mind and not by a conscious effort on the part of the communicator.

Q. 97

If the physical body has an etheric counterpart, is the next plane of existence the etheric counterpart of the earth? If so, what is the structure of the substance of which it is composed?

A.

The answer is no to the first part of the question. Know that all form manifestation has etheric counterparts. Thus, a tree has an etheric mould but is still part of your world, and this etheric `mould` is below the atomic vibration rate of our world. It is the SPIRIT that moves through the etheric realms and etheric forms, which are released as the entity rises above the plane of manifestation. Realise also that the etheric substance constantly returns to its atomic basis for reuse, similar in every way to the regeneration of substance in your world. The substance of our world is the same as yours but vibrating at a higher rate and producing more light, consequently, more under the influence of the mind.

Q. 98

Do all planets possess an etheric counterpart?

A.

Yes, everything which has form has an etheric element.

Q. 99

Please expand on "effects produced by the harmonics of the Group Soul" (A. 62)

A.

As the entity enters a harmonic relationship with the Group Soul, previous information and experience of others within the group becomes available, welling up from the deepest levels of consciousness and producing spiritual effects of sound and colour within the pilgrim. Other effects are involved which are beyond your understanding at the present time. See this in the sense of harmonic relationship, where separate entities are as one by the reciprocal vibrations produced.

Q. 100

Is there any special evolutionary reason for the massive difference in the standard of living that exists in various parts of the world?

A.

Certain environments produce greater pressures for evolutionary forces to press forward. Remember that necessity is the mother of invention and that difficult circumstances often produce the most striking results. It is more important to know that less advanced peoples in your world are just as essential to advancement and provide the polarity essential for progress. Thus, the advanced must pull up those who provide the information, who in turn and who alone can keep the seesaw of progress moving. Should the difference become too great, disruption can be expected.

Q. 101

Why is the experience in the first realm not vital? (A.63)

A.

It is vital, but not to any particular individual, as the one lives in all. Every entity is unique and different. If everything is vital, as you say, then there would be the need for only one entity. The fact that each one is unique shows that each performs a unique role whilst supplying group Soul and Central Source with experience gathered

Q. 102

What is the purpose of gathering information for the whole, and what will happen when the whole is complete?

A.

We can only assume that the whole is expanded and grows through the experiences gained. Our minds cannot go further, but it is possible that what we call the Central Source, or whole or God, is also part of another whole. Completion is when all are `gathered in` and is beyond our knowledge.

Q. 103

Please give details of the conditions prevailing in the level of experience before the earthly one.

A.

It is impossible to speak generally as this would be different for each entity. In your case, you rested within the Group Soul, bathing in the experience of your spiritual group.

Q. 104

Some people seem to go through this life thinking and caring only for themselves. They steal and perhaps commit murder, never giving thought to the anguish they cause others. How will they be treated after their transition?

A.

In accordance with the law of compensation and retribution. They will be brought into a situation where the will is strengthened and the weakness of their natures overcome. Those higher in the evolutionary process are responsible for these entities, and they are administered to by the Angels of Light. All life and manifestation are in a state of progress even when obscured as in the foregoing situation.

Q. 105

What is the cause of arthritis, and how can it be treated?

A.

This is a condition in which the body is unable to handle materials in the proper manner, and various conditions arise from this basic cause. The reaction of calcium through chemical imbalance produces material unable to consolidate and which prefers disintegration through various channels. Metabolic disturbances are involved hence the endocrine system and lymphatic and eliminative processes through excessive demands made upon them. Therapy directed towards metabolic consolidation and the complete elimination of waste matter will bring desired results.

Q 106

Could a more detailed description be given of an entity's emergence from the Central Source, through to its return to the same?

A.

The Source to the Group Soul, and thence into the stream of experience. Back to the group and thence to the Source.

Q. 107

If certain types of disease are caused by electrical imbalance at cellular levels, would it not be possible to alter or correct this by electrical means?

A.

The future will see this development of electro-magnetic therapy combined with other waveforms at present not understood in your world. Consider the various waveforms known to you and their ability to pass through your body. Combine this with new developments, and you will see the perfect tools for adjusting the body.

Q. 108

If diseases first manifest at microscopic or cellular levels, can they be detected in the auric colors before it manifests as physical signs and symptoms?

A.

Yes, but think more in terms of disturbances in the magnetic field rather than colour emanation, which are slower to manifest. Only when a complete electro-magnetic system of examination is developed can these ideas be of significance.

Q. 109

What opportunities are the spiritually unevolved given after transitioning in order to progress?

A.

Every opportunity which is necessary to make their lights shine through my presentation to their own negative condition, some remorse, etc., is to be expected. Also, know that progress is from within, and no one else may pay for the entity. Each must work their own passage.

Q. 110

If some type of music can be used to bring harmony and healing to the body, surely there must also be music or sound which has the opposite effect?

A.

Yes, that which causes the aura to retract, or contact is usually harmful, whilst good music causes expansion and strengthening of the auric field, by their `lights` shall ye know them.

Q. 111

Please give a description of the first type of existence experienced after being sent forth from the Central Source.

A.

Like yours, of earth life with a sublimated memory of the group soul, the latter being out of focus.

Q. 112

Please give advice to those seeking proof of survival.

A.

Beware that such is a special blessing bestowed in accordance with Divine Will. Approach with reverence the appointed place and time of the meeting, with a mind which is carefully attuned to the spiritual universe. Be as a child,

311

expect to receive, and the door will be opened, if in accordance with Divine Will. Remember that your communication is via the spirit medium, and care should be taken to ensure that a proper connection is made to the medium. This is where most communications are obstructed.

Q. 113

Please enlarge about cancer.

A.

A disease of civilisation more connected to the sins of modern living than generally appreciated. The effects to the endocrine system of refined foods and the removal of essential items of roughage, fresh fruit, vegetables, etc., are to be largely thought of as connecting with this condition. Also, meat-eating may have a bad effect upon the system through aura conditions prevailing prior to the slaughter of animals. i.e., you are literally eating fear!

Q. 114

What is the effect of vitamin C upon the malignant tissue?

A.

Obviously, ascorbic acid is the polarity of alkaline balance, as previously stated. Thus, the electro-magnetic field is stimulated, according to other conditions; it can impede or accelerate the growth rate. More research is needed here. Often combined with other substances and will cause a temporary hold of the cancer cells, which may then accelerate with greater speed than before the Vitamin C was administered.

Q. 115

Do physical causes contribute to malignant change in the body? i.e., car cinegenic substances, radiation, and chronic infection?

A.

Yes, mainly from the physical too much stress placed upon psychosomatic causes. Keep research mainly in the physical field where most causes are. All life and manifestation are in a state of radiation, and you may know that even the radiation of the sun's rays may cause malignancy to develop, where surrounding conditions are right for this to happen. About infection, it depends entirely upon the infection which is present. Probably with the certain infective condition, the side products may even impede the cancer cells through accidental immunisation into the cell tissue of antibodies from the infection. This may provide a future therapy for treatment in established cases.

Q. 116

Is it possible to immunise against malignancy?

A.

Look to hormone therapy and the possibility of linking this concept to endocrine therapy by chemical engineering of hormones through synthesis with known resisting agents.

Q. 117

Please expand on the previous answer.

A.

Many endocrine substances are twinned in their activity, stimulating or subduing other polarities within the system. See the same, acid/alkaline, electrical/magnetic balance is demonstrated. Particularly the pituitary hormones, where the anterior and posterior pituitary substances have a definite role in cancer conditions. Relate to the previous answer, therefore, to the pituitary hormone concerned with growth and its twinned hormonal partner, and you have a starting point before you.

Q. 118

What methods could be used to monitor the hormonal changes within the body?

A.

Start with known techniques for examination of same through blood sampling with reference to the latest development in spectrograph and microspectroscopic analysis.

Q. 119

Please give a step-by-step account of the changes which occur in tissue undergoing malignant change.

A.

Extremely difficult because we could produce pages and pages of changes for you, but we will start with the first change which occurs within the genetic code of the cell caused by an alteration of the electrical circuit, and then by an alteration of the magnetic field, a new blueprint is produced for the tissue to follow. Thus, the etheric blueprint, through the primary change in the genetic code, is established. Take the genetic material which emanates its own etheric blueprint and aura, a mould into which the body pours its cells and materials. We mean to say that the body can only follow the form and shape which is already established, though invisible, at the etheric level.

Q. 120

Are the causes of benign neoplasms different from those of malignant ones?

A.

Yes, but quite simply, one is the positive polarity, and the other is negative. In benign tumours, negative polarity is manifested, and in malignant cases, it is positive. One grows through positive acceleration; the other simply "coats" the etheric mould.

Q.121

If the endocrine system holds the key to malignant change in the body, how can one ensure that this system is kept in the best possible condition?

A.

Not "the key but a key" ("the" tends to limit the viewing of other contributory factors.) the endocrine system is largely imbalanced already in the world by hereditary forces. This imbalance is on the increase and not decreasing. Each new generation will bring an increase in the endocrine imbalance, as where both parents are imbalanced, their offspring will surely be imbalanced as well. Look to the stimulation of the system with short meter waves, a la Samuels and further research la Lakhovsky.

Q. 122

Can any advice be given in order to stimulate the pancreas of an insulin-dependent diabetic to a state where it can once again produce enough insulin for the body's needs?

A.

It is already known that cases have been recorded where a shock to the system has caused a "sleeping" pancreas to "awaken". Remember that it is simply a matter of a "factory" closing because the working programmer was too heavy, and it closes to prevent the strain from passing back through the system to more vital areas. However, once the conditions have been evident for some time, the electrical force is withdrawn from the cells, and effective regeneration of the organ will pose special difficulties. It is probable that the use of sonic radiation may prove of greatest value in the future as the sound vibration of this organ is very dominant. More of this area of investigation with the use of sound waves is already taking place by your medical researchers. Sound irradiation and not electrical stimulation may bring the best results.

Q. 123

Advice on sound, please!

A.

Sound is the basis of form. Please include this in your cancer questions and know that sound could be applied effectively in both illnesses. To start and to avoid overstimulation in music, which is enjoyed, could be used to form a wide blanket of vibrations across the area without the risk of danger indicated.

Q. 124

Do other members of the Group Soul live on earth at the present time?

A.

Yes, there are at the present time five spirits in the earth world from this group.

Q. 125

Who are they?

A.

There are three on your island of Great Britain. X.X and Y.Y are two, and another exists a further two live in other parts of the world, and you will not join with them during this mission.

Who is spirit Ron Baker? He was a respected spirit medium who I believe was a president of St. Helens spiritual church, Northwest of England. I was given his thesis that you have seen, and at the time when I was reading, I had a sense that Ron was at my side. I never had the chance to meet Ron Baker when he was here on the earth. Nevertheless, meeting him in the spirit of communication is an inspiration. I had the impression from Ron that he would like me to contribute his automatic writing, so others can experience and learn from them.

My spiritual intelligence allows me to accept the content of Spirit Ron Bakers' automatic writing through his physical mediumship. It is also important that you should have an open mind about spiritual activities, and before anything, all explanations should be examined of the likelihood of the cause. I today still look for a simple explanation, and when there isn't any, then and only then I will accept the spiritual activity as, in fact, happened.

It is every spiritual person's duty to examine all spirit communication events regardless of how long you have been aware of spirit communication. There is no room for fabricated spirit communication. It only feeds your ego, which is not part of a spiritual matter.

Thank you to pioneers like Mr Ron Baker for helping us to understand spirit communication and teaching us how close the two worlds are. I salute you for your dedication, commitment, and honesty. You have inspired me from the day I first read your wonderful Journal. And I look forward to the time when we meet will meet again.

Summary

To conclude this manual, it is important for me to stress that every person has the psychic ability to create spirit communication. We were all born with the sixth sense, some people choose to develop, and others simply have forgotten about their psychic senses, maybe because they live in the form world and use their physical senses.

This book does not only help you to develop your psychic abilities, but it is also a book to broaden your spiritual knowledge. It will certainly provide you with food for thought. Whatever your reasons are for purchasing this book, I know you will certainly see a change in your thoughts. You will have more of an understanding. You will see that your spirit, family and friends are only a thoughtful way because energy continues. When the physical body dies, your energy will find another vehicle to express itself.

I have endeavoured to provide information that will enhance the beginnings of spiritual phenomena or spiritual knowledge for the seeker. You must understand developing your spiritual/psychic senses dedication and a lifetime commitment. You must establish a working partnership with

320

the unseen hosts who may be drawn to you at the early stages of development.

Your sixth sense development will start off at a slow pace and increase as time goes by. Your development cannot be forced or rushed. The unseen hosts will decide when the time is correct to move forward, so it is important to understand it is not a race of speed but a marathon.

You must have an open, cleared mind at all attempts of linking to the energy source. If you have not, the unseen host will find it difficult to pass the wall you have created. Therefore, the first phase of developing with be analysing the past contents, learning who you are, and not what you think you are. Look at it like emptying the garbage, removing the rubbish, and there is no one with a full dustbin or trash can. Examine all spirit communication. They will test you, and being honest with yourself is very important.

Fear of the unknown holds people back from discovering their true self Fear of the unknown, basically anything we don't understand we create fear, which is mainly due to lack of knowledge, especially about the unknown. Spiritual knowledge eliminates fear. It brings an understanding of spiritual phenomena, and when we understand it encourages us to seek more spiritual information. This book aims to remove all fears and encourage you to seek further spiritual information for your personal satisfaction.

You will have spiritual information, and the knowledge will dispel some of the evil entity or ghost stories, which is created to control certain religious groups or by the movie industry to gain profit. You will also have more of an understanding of what happens at death or what happens to us when we die. Your thoughts will change, giving you peace of mind knowing your family members or friends have made the transition to a higher vibrational world, higher than the earth's vibrations.

Every religion quotes spirit in their doctrines their holy books. Being a spiritual person has no judgement on people's different beliefs. We all have opinion and choices, which is accepted by a spiritual seeker. Spiritual is for everyone, and everyone is equal. Being spiritual is being in tune with all life forms of the earth. And it is your duty of care for the creator of life and the planet that we live on, which is only temporarily.

I know this can be hard for you to understand, but hopefully, this book will bring you some understanding and help you to grow your inner spirit. Once you become accustomed to the connecting energy source, you will find your life will become easier. You will start to think more of your spiritual life and not your life situation. When you are asked about your life, you will tell them who you are and about your spiritual life, instead of mentioning your life situation, paying the bills, not looking forward to, following the same daily routine, the stress of life situations. You will be free of all the latter, or you will organise your life situation, so you put yourself first and do the things you want to do. You will be taking control of your life.

When you start to develop your spiritual/psychic gift, the unseen host will know which type of spirit communication will be suited for you by your physical body chemicals, energies, and your electro-magnetic field. You often hear mystics say they are a spiritual healer, a psychic, a spirit medium, or say I am a clairvoyant, or I work with higher energies. Sorry to disappoint. These thoughts only lead to public ridicule and disillusion of the true spiritual connection. These kinds of thoughts only hamper true spiritual teachings. Therefore this sort of quote needs to be dispelled. Maybe these people are underdeveloped, and they should go back to the development stages and stay for a while longer, in my opinion.

During your development, you will find a relationship between you and the unseen host will develop and at some point, you will know their name. The name they used on the earth, in my opinion, is usually someone who knew you, maybe a family member or a friend. It could be a group of spirit helpers. Whoever they are, you will know? Please do not make up a spirit name to fulfil your ego. It is being honest to yourself and to your unseen hosts.

If you are seeking to develop your psychic senses, you must understand it is a lifetime commitment on earth and in the energy world. When you pass to the energy world of spirit, you will still be working as a spirit helper, which would be decided the moment you are in transition. Your task will be to help your fellow man while on earth, look after the animals of the earth, and help to take care of nature.

It can be a difficult task to reach people on a mental or physical level. However, on a spiritual level, they can be reached, and that's where the marvellous work takes place. Whatever your reasons are, you will be walking high with the knowledge of knowing your life does continue in a higher dimension that no one can fully understand until it is time for us to move on.

When you have finished reading this book, you will have your own thoughts, opinions, views, and that is fine. My aim is not to promote my beliefs on you but to help to provide you with food for thought, in other words, to point you in the direction of seeking further knowledge. My personal spiritual experience would be of no benefit to you, and it would be totally impossible for me to explain them. When you have your spiritual experiences, then you will learn to understand the true meaning of what I am trying to convey in this book.

I have entered my spiritual encounters that would hopefully help you of your way to develop your spiritual senses and bring you to seek further intuition on this remarkable subject. If my book manages to help one soul, then it was worthwhile spending time writing.